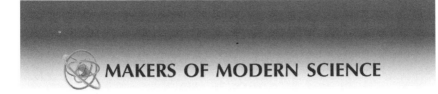

MAKERS OF MODERN SCIENCE

Alan
Turing

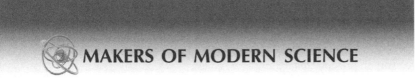

MAKERS OF MODERN SCIENCE

Alan Turing

*Computing Genius and
Wartime Code Breaker*

HARRY HENDERSON

CHELSEA HOUSE
PUBLISHERS
An imprint of Infobase Publishing

Alan Turing: Computing Genius and Wartime Code Breaker

Copyright © 2011 by Harry Henderson

Chelsea House
An imprint of Infobase Publishing
132 West 31st Street
New York NY 10001

Library of Congress Cataloging-in-Publication Data

Henderson, Harry, 1951–
    Alan Turing : computing genius and wartime code breaker / Harry Henderson.
        p. cm.—(Makers of modern science)
    Includes bibliographical references and index.
    ISBN 978-0-8160-6175-4
    1. Turing, Alan Mathison, 1912–1954—Juvenile literature. 2. Mathematicians—Great Britain—Biography—Juvenile literature. I. Title. II. Series.
    QA29.T8H46. 2011
    510.92—dc22   2010015798

Chelsea House books are available at special discounts when purchased in bulk quantities for businesses, associations, institutions, or sales promotions. Please call our Special Sales Department in New York at (212) 967-8800 or (800) 322-8755.

You can find Chelsea House on the World Wide Web at
http://www.chelseahouse.com

Text design by Kerry Casey
Composition by Keith Trego
Illustrations by Sholto Ainslie
Photo research by Suzanne M. Tibor
Cover printed by Art Print, Taylor, Pa.
Book printed and bound by Maple Press, York, Pa.
Date printed: February 2011
Printed in the United States of America

10 9 8 7 6 5 4 3 2 1

This book is printed on acid-free paper.

For Will and Thad
In gratitude for many hours of
universal human conversation

CONTENTS

PREFACE

....

Science is, above all, a great human adventure. It is the process of exploring what Albert Einstein called the "magnificent structure" of nature using observation, experience, and logic. Science comprises the best methods known to humankind for finding reliable answers about the unknown. With these tools, scientists probe the great mysteries of the universe—from black holes and star nurseries to deep-sea hydrothermal vents (and extremophile organisms that survive high temperatures to live in them); from faraway galaxies to subatomic particles such as quarks and antiquarks; from signs of life on other worlds to microorganisms such as bacteria and viruses here on Earth; from how a vaccine works to protect a child from disease to the DNA, genes, and enzymes that control traits and processes from the color of a boy's hair to how he metabolizes sugar.

Some people think that science is rigid and static, a dusty, musty set of facts and statistics to memorize for a test and then forget. Some think of science as antihuman—devoid of poetry, art, and a sense of mystery. However, science is based on a sense of wonder and is all about exploring the mysteries of life and our planet and the vastness of the universe. Science offers methods for testing and reasoning that help keep us honest with ourselves. As physicist Richard Feynman once said, science is above all a way to keep from fooling yourself—or letting nature (or others) fool you. Nothing could be more growth-oriented or more human. Science evolves continually. New bits of knowledge and fresh discoveries endlessly shed light and open perspectives. As a result, science is constantly undergoing revolutions—ever refocusing what scientists have explored before into fresh, new understanding. Scientists like to say science is self-correcting. That is, science is fallible, and scientists can be wrong. It is easy to fool yourself, and it is easy to be fooled by others, but because new facts are constantly flowing in, scientists are continually refining their work to account for as many facts as possible. So science can make mistakes, but it also can correct itself.

Sometimes, as medical scientist Jonas Salk liked to point out, good science thrives when scientists ask the right question about what they observe. "What people think of as the moment of discovery is really the discovery of the question," he once remarked.

There is no one, step-by-step "scientific method" that all scientists use. However, science requires the use of methods that are systematic, logical, and *empirical* (based on objective observation and experience). The goal of science is to explore and understand how nature works—what causes the patterns, the shapes, the colors, the textures, the consistency, the mass, and all the other characteristics of the natural universe that we see.

What is it like to be a scientist? Many people think of stereotypes of the scientist trapped in cold logic or the cartoonlike "mad" scientists. In general, these portrayals are more imagination than truth. Scientists use their brains. They are exceptionally good at logic and critical thinking. This is where the generalizations stop. Although science follows strict rules, it is often guided by the many styles and personalities of the scientists themselves, who have distinct individuality, personality, and style. What better way to explore what science is all about than through the experiences of great scientists?

Each volume of the Makers of Modern Science series presents the life and work of a prominent scientist whose outstanding contributions have garnered the respect and recognition of the world. These men and women were all great scientists, but they differed in many ways. Their approaches to the use of science were different: Niels Bohr was an atomic theorist whose strengths lay in patterns, ideas, and conceptualization, while Wernher von Braun was a hands-on scientist/engineer who led the team that built the giant rocket used by Apollo astronauts to reach the Moon. Some's genius was sparked by solitary contemplation—geneticist Barbara McClintock worked alone in fields of maize and sometimes spoke to no one all day long. Others worked as members of large, coordinated teams. Oceanographer Robert Ballard organized oceangoing ship crews on submersible expeditions to the ocean floor; biologist Jonas Salk established the

Salk Institute to help scientists in different fields collaborate more freely and study the human body through the interrelationships of their differing knowledge and approaches. Their personal styles also differed: biologist Rita Levi-Montalcini enjoyed wearing chic dresses and makeup; McClintock was sunburned and wore baggy denim jeans and an oversized shirt; nuclear physicist Richard Feynman was a practical joker and an energetic bongo drummer.

The scientists chosen represent a spectrum of disciplines and a diversity of approaches to science as well as lifestyles. Each biography explores the scientist's younger years along with education and growth as a scientist; the experiences, research, and contributions of the maturing scientist; and the course of the path to recognition. Each volume also explores the nature of science and its unique usefulness for studying the universe and contains sidebars covering related facts or profiles of interest, introductory coverage of the scientist's field, line illustrations and photographs, a time line, a glossary of related scientific terms, and a list of further resources including books, Web sites, periodicals, and associations.

The volumes in the Makers of Modern Science series offer a factual look at the lives and exciting contributions of the profiled scientists in the hope that readers will see science as a uniquely human quest to understand the universe and that some readers may be inspired to follow in the footsteps of these great scientists.

ACKNOWLEDGMENTS

I would like to thank my editor, Frank K. Darmstadt, for his patient help and suggestions, Suzie Tibor for her hard work in rounding up the photographs, and as always my wife, Lisa Yount.

INTRODUCTION

The term *code* can refer to several different things. One is the secret code or cipher that is used to conceal a message from anyone except the person intended to receive it. Today, cryptography, the science of secure communications, is an essential part of our daily lives. Among other things, encryption protects our credit card information when we buy something online.

Codes of Concealment

During World War II, cryptology and cryptanalysis (the "breaking" of codes and ciphers) came of age. Alan Turing, the subject of this book in the Makers of Modern Science set, did more than anyone else to make sure that Britain and its ally the United States would be able to survive the initial Nazi onslaught long enough to assemble the mighty armada and invading army that would lead to victory. Chapter 4 will show how Turing, building on the work of earlier code breakers, applied innovative mathematical techniques to decrypting the messages from German Enigma cipher machines. Eventually, another German cipher machine would be defeated by a British machine called Colossus that could scan and analyze messages electronically.

The ultimate significance of Colossus could only be understood because a decade earlier Turing had tackled one of the toughest problems in pure mathematics. In order to prove his theorem about the fundamental nature of computation, Turing imagined a "universal machine" that could perform any possible computation by combining a few simple instructions and using an endless "memory" consisting of a paper tape. Chapter 3 explores the remarkably long history of mechanical computation and then shows how Turing, along with the American logician Alonzo Church, laid the mathematical groundwork for the modern computer.

Computer Code and Artificial Intelligence

After the war, Turing had the opportunity to work on several pioneering computer projects that would make the universal machine a physical reality. Focusing mainly on software rather than hardware, Turing developed instruction sets and program routines whose descendants are found today in the latest computer microprocessors. These machine instructions would give a second meaning to the word *code.* Today, a large program such as the Windows operating system can consist of more than 50 million lines of code. Chapter 5 looks at the problems faced by the first computer designers and the role Turing played in extending the potential of these early machines.

If Turing had stopped there, he would already have been both a genuine (if unconventional) war hero and one of the most important computer pioneers. However, even while he was working on practical computer projects, Turing's remarkable mind was ranging far afield and ahead to topics that seemed to be sheer science fiction. In particular, Turing was the first to write in detail about the possibility of a machine showing true intelligence.

In a remarkable paper, "Intelligent Machinery," Turing asked how one could tell whether a computer was truly intelligent. The experiment he proposed, now called the Turing test, was deceptively simple. It would pit a human being against an unknown entity, communicating over a teletype line. Turing suggested that if a computer program could converse in a sufficiently humanlike way to fool the human into thinking another person was on the line, that program would have to be acknowledged to be what we now call an artificial intelligence, or AI. Chapter 6 shows how Turing developed this and other ideas while replying to the objections of theologians, mathematicians, philosophers, and others who argue that no machine could cross the divide separating sentient humans from mindless gadgets.

Genetic Code

Turing's restless and fertile mind then seemed to be on the verge of yet another field of discovery. This involved another kind of code—what would be known as the genetic code. Although the role of DNA in carrying and structuring that code would not be known until after Turing's death, Turing developed a promising form of mathematical biology that sought to explain patterns of growth in organisms. While he applied his ideas to relatively simple examples such as the branching of plants and the spots on cows, his ultimate goal was to understand that most complex of biological structures, the human brain.

As is recounted in chapter 7, Turing's work toward this goal and the possibility of even more fields of scientific exploration would be tragically cut short. The master of wartime codes, machine codes, and potential genetic codes would ultimately endure a fateful (and perhaps fatal) collision with yet another kind of code.

Human Code

The term *code* can also refer to a system of laws or morals that regulate behavior. As chapter 1 shows, even as a boy and a young preparatory school student, Turing inevitably clashed with conventional codes of behavior. His brilliant mind was housed in a rather awkward (if sometimes energetic) body. He did not fit into an environment that often seemed to value sports, teamwork, and social conformity over intellectual achievement.

As he grew older, Turing became increasingly aware that he was "different" from most men around him, down to his very genetic code. He accepted that he was a homosexual, and struggled to find a handful of friends who would accept him in turn. But in his exploration of the gay underground of Manchester, England, he would run afoul of a final code, the British legal code that made homosexual contact a felony.

Enduring arrest, trial, and medical treatment for his homosexuality, Turing appeared to be on the verge of a new life when he was found dead, in a scene from a fairy tale, with an apparently poisoned apple by his side. Turing was not yet 42 years old.

Although his life was cut short by tragedy, Alan Turing left a legacy written in decrypted messages, computer architecture and programming, biological patterns, and astonishing possibilities for the future of intelligence.

An Unusual Child

Alan Mathison Turing was born June 23, 1912, in London, England, when his brother John was five. The two boys grew up during those early years in the absence of their parents. For Alan's birth, though, Julius Turing and his wife, the former Ethel Sara Stoney, had come home on furlough from India. Their first son had been born in Madras; the second, they were determined, would come into the world on British soil.

Alan Turing's mother and father both came from a family background of "empire builders" in India. At the time, India was still part of a world-spanning British Empire—indeed, it was considered the jewel of that empire. However it was a deeply troubled jewel, where millions suffered in extreme poverty and an independence movement was being organized by Mohandas (or Mahatma)

Gandhi (1869–1948), using nonviolent but effective tactics of civil disobedience.

The Turings' connection with India went back a generation to Victorian times. Alan's maternal grandfather was chief engineer of the Madras Railway, and his mother had lived in India much of her life. When Alan was born, his father had already worked in India for 10 years. During the early years of Alan's life, from 1912 to 1926, Julius and Sara Turing lived primarily in India, with only brief visits back to England and a few family trips for vacations.

Despite their focus on public service, both families also achieved some fame in science and mathematics. In 1891, a distant relative of Sara's, the Irish physicist George Johnstone Stoney (1826–1911), had named the atomic particle known today as an electron. (At the time, the particle was theoretical, but the Cambridge University physicist J. J. Thomson [1856–1940] physically discovered it six years later). Sara took pride in this and even greater pride in her relative's membership in the Royal Society, one of the most prestigious scientific bodies in the world.

On the paternal side of the family, Julius's father had earned a degree in mathematics, placing 11th in his class at Trinity College, one of the most respected schools at Cambridge University, which was an icon in the field of pure mathematics. However, despite the honors he had won, Alan's grandfather had not pursued an academic career.

Absent Parents

In the early decades of the 20th century, many upper-middle-class British parents chose to leave the intellectual education and moral upbringing of their children to nannies in the early years, followed by a series of boarding schools.

For the Turings, the arrangement was for a couple of family friends, Colonel and Mrs. Ward, to foster the boys. The Wards lived at St. Leonards-on-Sea, near Hastings in southeastern England. While the colonel took little direct interest in the lives of the young Turings, they soon became fond of Mrs. Ward, whom they called Grannie. However, the actual day-to-day care of the boys was the responsibility of Nanny Thompson. Thompson was also their first teacher. For the Turing boys, life with the Wards would be occasionally interrupted by the temporary return of their parents to England.

According to Andrew Hodges (1949–   ) in his biography of Turing, Nanny Thompson later recalled Turing as a boy with unusual characteristics. "The thing that stands out most in my mind was his *integrity* and his *intelligence* for a child so young as he then was." Playing games with him, she would sometimes try to arrange for him to win, but she said he always refused to bend the rules in that way. He may also have taken this stance out of pride, refusing the condescension. He wanted to win on his own.

Even as a young boy, Alan stood out in attitude and behavior. Alan resisted other people's attempts to draw him into the prevailing systems—whether at home or in school. He talked back and at least hinted that he could cause trouble. According to Hodges, as Alan's mother prepared in 1915 to leave the boys behind once again and head for Madras and reunion with her husband, she murmured to Alan, "You'll be a good boy, won't you?" He was about three years old. "Yes," came Alan's reply, "but sometimes I shall forget."

Even before he was old enough to go to his first school, Alan taught himself to read, though his greatest enthusiasm seemed to be reserved for numbers. When he was six, he was enrolled in St. Michael's day school, where the headmistress remarked on the boy's mathematical talent.

Turing as a boy of five (King's College Archive Centre, Cambridge; the Papers of Alan Mathison Turing)

As he grew up, the independent-minded Alan liked to pursue the tough problems, the ones that no one else could figure out how to do. He felt that school imposed on his time and interrupted his own projects—such as testing substances and reactions with his chemistry set, collecting maps, researching genealogy, poring over science books, and organizing chess tournaments.

Hazelhurst

In 1922, Alan followed his brother, John, to enroll in Hazelhurst, a small preparatory school for about 36 boys, ages 9 to 11.

One of Alan's teachers said he had genius; others would become annoyed by his leaps ahead to get to the interesting part of an assignment. Regardless, the job at hand was to prepare for the entrance exam for public school. (*Public school* is the British term for what in the United States would be called a private college preparatory school.) The curriculum focused on passing the Common Entrance examination—especially the Latin test (considered a critical, key subject at the time)—and the rest of the prerequisites for entering public school.

According to Hodges, pictures of Alan from that year looked melancholy and wan. Some biographers have conjectured that, since he was fond of his mother, who was hardly ever around, he was naturally despondent. Others postulate that he wanted to study what he wanted and to explore the ideas and projects that interested him— not a preset curriculum focused on cramming information into his cranium to pass a test. He was not lazy, but school did bore him.

His interests lay elsewhere—particularly in science. Alan was 10, but he seemed to be world-weary already, as well as bored and lonely. At that time, he had no real friends. He and his brother, who was considerably more sociable, lived a drab life with the gruff colonel and his wife. Mrs. Ward complained that the boys did not like to play war games and accused Alan in particular of being a bookworm. His mother chided him for this in her letters from halfway around the world. There were occasionally other children boarding with the Wards, and the couple's own children were there, but Alan did not take to any of them.

For entertainment, Alan and John sometimes went to the movies or to the nearby beaches. Family vacations brought the boys and parents together occasionally—in Scotland and later in St. Moritz, Switzerland, where the two boys learned to ski. Eventually, John asked his father to find another home, which Julius agreed to do, and that made their childhood a little more pleasant.

Finally, at Hazelhurst, Alan apparently realized that he needed to catch up in the basics, and he taught himself to write. In due time, he passed the entrance exam to public school and he registered at Sherborne School in southern England.

Sherborne School

From the start, there were doubts about whether young Alan Turing was really suitable for public school life. As quoted by Hodges, the headmaster of Sherborne School told Julius that:

> *I hope he will not fall between two stools. If he is to stay at Public School, he must aim at becoming educated. If he is to be solely a Scientific Specialist, he is wasting his time at a Public School*

(By "educated" the headmaster meant the traditional course of study of the British public school, which emphasized the classics (Latin and Greek) as well as what we now call liberal arts.)

Despite his possible unsuitability for such an institution, Julius chose Sherborne School for the beginning of Alan's formal education.

Like many other prestigious British public schools, Sherborne had roots that went back centuries. The little country town where Sherborne School still reigns was the location of one of the first Christian sites, including the abbey, which was founded in the eighth century and is still in use by the school. In 1550, the school was designated for local education, and in 1896, Sherborne became a boarding school for boys. Some of the school's buildings remained from the original school. After some ups and downs, by 1926 a new headmaster doubled the number of students to 400 and boosted the school's reputation—just about the time the Turings were looking for a school for their younger son.

In the 1920s, according to biographer Andrew Hodges, the school was considered at least "moderately distinguished." Alan's father and mother felt considerably relieved when Alan gained entrance to Sherborne, since admission was highly competitive.

As Alan's mother tells her biography of Alan,

> *Though he had been loved and understood in the narrower homely circle of his preparatory school, it was because I foresaw the possible difficulties for the staff and himself at a public school that I was at such pains to find the right one for him, lest if he failed in adaptation to public school he might become a mere intellectual crank.*

An Intrepid Journey

In the meantime, without warning, Julius Turing suddenly took an early retirement when authorities passed over him for an advancement that he felt should have been his. In his view, he had earned it and he considered himself better qualified than the appointee. So, after more than two decades of a solid career, he had left the Indian civil service. Julius and Sara made their last trip back to England from India, and, to avoid English taxes, they settled with their two boys in the town of Dinard in Brittany, located in the northwest corner of France where it juts out into the Atlantic Ocean. From Brittany, Alan and John would travel across the English Channel to England, where they would board at their respective schools during the school term.

When he disembarked in the port of Southampton after crossing the English Channel, the younger Turing heard that no trains, buses, or taxis were in use because of a nationwide transportation strike. So, he simply began rearranging the final stage of his trip. He took his bicycle from his baggage at the port, bought a map, and pedaled the 60 miles or so northeast from the port to the school, stopping along the way twice for bicycle repairs. He took the opportunity and spent the night at an upscale hotel (a decision that his father would not have approved, but then, Julius was not there). Alan kept careful track of the costs for his parents and mailed home his receipts and change.

On his arrival at Sherborne, the faculty and other students were amazed to see him pedaling up to the campus, arriving right on time despite the lockdown, and he gained admiration for his resourcefulness.

Public School Life

As a student in school, however, Alan Turing was much less impressive. Indeed, he was a mess: illegible handwriting, scratchy and leaky pen points, and a shirt that was rarely tucked in. Despite

The Public School in British Culture

In Britain and other British Commonwealth countries, a "public school" is a privately funded institution that charges tuition fees. It is "public" in the sense that it is open to any student who qualifies and can afford it, but in practice British public schools have generally drawn their students from the upper classes.

Most public schools are boarding schools where students live for the duration of the school term. The years covered are generally (in American terms) junior high through high school.

The traditional British public school was a single-sex (boys only) environment. There was a strong emphasis on sports, particularly soccer (known as football in Britain) and cricket. Academically, the emphasis was on the classics (Greek and Roman language and culture) and studies intended to prepare students for college, followed by careers in the military or colonial administration. Because the graduate was expected to become a gentleman and an officer or official, studies that involved practical subjects such as science, industry, or business were neglected.

The public school of the 19th and early 20th centuries was a harsh environment for anyone who did not fit in. Bullying was common, and older boys were expected to physically discipline younger students for any infractions of school rules. In an environment virtually free of female influence, a sort of exaggerated masculinity often resulted. At the same time, intense friendships were often formed between boys, including homosexual relationships.

his mathematical aptitude, he could not do long division, and he stammered in a high, squeaky voice when he talked.

Turing's report cards soon reflected his teachers' exasperation. For example:

> *I can forgive his writing, though it is the worst I have ever seen, and I try to view tolerantly his unswerving inexactitude and slipshod, dirty, work, inconsistent though such inexactitude is in a utilitarian; but I cannot forgive the stupidity of his attitude towards sane discussion on the New Testament.*

In English, Turing was at the very bottom of his class. In Latin, which was considered necessary for any educated person, Turing stood a little better—second from the bottom.

Alan was, by most reports, a lonely, unsociable boy with few friends. Sometimes he apparently forgot that he lived in a world where children were to be seen and not heard.

Alan continued to study the esoteric, challenging problems he liked, and he often did poorly in school tests because he was always looking ahead in his textbooks, paying no attention to basics. It was one of his teachers' biggest complaints.

Flashes of Genius

At first, Sherborne seemed as impossible to bear as Hazelhurst had been. Reports about Turing's progress were mixed. His teachers tended to bear down on the most troublesome issues, without acknowledging his strong points, of which there were many. For example, at 15, Turing worked out the mathematical formulas for the inverse tangent function. Admittedly, someone else had already figured this out, but nonetheless he was still working with material that was well beyond the level of his classmates, and he had derived this formula on his own.

In chemistry, at 14, Turing had figured out a method for extracting iodine from seaweed gathered from the beaches near the new family home in Dinard. The chemistry instructor was amazed at the advanced level this inconspicuous boy had reached all on his own. Another teacher commented that Alan "thinks very rapidly and is apt to be 'brilliant.'"

Indeed, chemistry would become a lifelong pursuit of Turing's, even though he did not enter the field professionally. He spent hours tinkering with chemicals, trying to build elaborate combinations and reactions from the kinds of simple substances one might find around the house.

Turing at the age of 16 (King's College Archive Centre, Cambridge; the Papers of Alan Mathison Turing)

Most reports made to parents by teachers, though, were complaints. Besides the usual complaints about sloppy handwriting, the chief complaint was that while Turing's work frequently showed signs of brilliance, it was not methodical or orderly. In mathematics, particularly, the approved method was to build a proof step by step, making sure that each conclusion is justified by what has been proven before. Turing's housemaster, however, said that the boy's approach was like "trying to build a roof before he has laid the foundations."

The Discovery of Friendship

At Sherborne, however, Alan finally found a friend—Christopher Morcom, who liked science as much as Alan did. Morcom's mother was an artist, trained at the Sorbonne (a part of the University of Paris devoted to the arts and sciences). She had an apartment/studio in London, where she worked on sculpture and other art forms.

So, as it turned out, luckily, Alan's genius helped him to find a good friend at last who shared his interests in subjects that had no meaning to most people. The two had the same urge to devise and carry out relatively serious scientific experiments that challenged them both, and they competed against each other and taught each other the structures and beauty of science and logic.

Morcom and Turing had long discussions about Einstein's theories, during which Turing liked to point out how using real-world examples, such as a clock, helped Einstein bolster his arguments. (Turing even came up with a succinct formulation of the implication of Einstein's theories of general and special relativity for the motion of a particle.)

The two boys also liked to take up problems that they knew had recently been posed in the scientific community and then set out to compete with the pros. Morcom had a telescope at his family's lavish residence in the country (his family was wealthy thanks to their successful engineering firm), and he invited Turing to make use of it.

Turing could be said to have had a crush on Morcom. Such intense same-sex friendships are not uncommon among teens, and they do not necessarily have a sexual component. Nonetheless, Turing was becoming aware that he was sexually attracted to other boys rather than to girls. (If Turing made any tentative advances to Morcom, they appear to have been rejected, but without ending the friendship.)

Morcom was short and thin—smaller than Turing although he was a year older. He was also a year ahead of Turing in school, and not surprisingly, Morcom made higher scores when exam results were announced for the Higher School Certificate in 1929. Turing came in at 1033 in mathematics, while Morcom earned a substantially better score of 1436.

Despite the difference in age and the test scores, in December 1929, when Morcom took exams for entrance to college at Cambridge, Turing also signed up. The exams lasted several days, so the prospective students gathered in the evenings for card games or discussions. It was an exciting time for this intellectually elite group of young men—bright, informed, and confident. The very air seemed sweet and filled with promise for the future.

When the students took turns making up songs about one another, the verse for Turing went like this:

> *The maths brain lies often awake in his bed*
> *Doing logs to ten places and trig in his head*

Turing was hoping that he might gain entrance to college early, especially if Morcom passed and would be moving on. He knew the plan was a long shot, but he had to try. As expected, Morcom passed, earning a scholarship for his scores. Turing failed to pass, though, and would have to spend another year at Sherborne. Despite that fact, Turing would later say that those few winter days at Cambridge in 1929 were the best in his life.

Death of a Friend

However, this special time in two young lives would not last. During the Christmas and New Year's break of 1929–30, Turing and Morcom worked on various projects and exchanged letters, reporting results and comparing academic plans.

At the end of the break, the new term began smoothly enough, but as Hodges recounts, on February 6, 1930, after they had gone to a concert together, and Turing had returned to his room, during the night he awoke suddenly. He looked at the stars and the setting moon, and inexplicably thought "good-bye to Morcom."

On that same night, Morcom suddenly became dangerously ill. An emergency ambulance raced to pick him up and carry him off to a nearby hospital in London. Unknown to Turing, Morcom had suffered a childhood case of bovine tuberculosis from which he had never truly recovered. Everyone—both those who knew of his illness and those who did not—was shocked when he died just a few days later at the hospital, on February 13, 1930.

Turing was devastated at the loss of Morcom. He was certain he would never care for anyone as much or feel such a oneness with any other person. Nevertheless, life would have to go on. Indeed, Turing

The "Nature of Spirit"

After Christopher Morcom's death, Turing maintained a close friendship with Morcom's mother, sometimes going on trips with her and frequently writing to her. Meanwhile, he felt that Morcom was in some sense still present, perhaps living through Turing's own thoughts. To explain his ideas about life and death to Mrs. Morcom, Turing wrote a little paper called "Nature of Spirit."

Turing first seized on an idea that was sweeping through the scientific community, though its implications were scarcely known to religious people, philosophers, or the educated public. Turing had begun to study the new quantum theory in physics, and one of its discoveries was, in Turing's words, that "when we are dealing with atoms and electrons we are quite unable to know the exact state of them; the instruments [for observation] being made of atoms and electrons themselves."

From this idea, formulated by the German physicist Werner Heisenberg as the Uncertainty Principle, Turing concluded that human actions, too, could not be solely determined by physical causation. He suggested that "We have a will which is able to determine the actions of the atoms probably in a small portion of the brain, or possibly all over it. The rest of the body acts so as to amplify this."

This "will" might be evidence that what Turing called spirit is intimately connected to, but separate from, the body. He suggests:

resolved that he would undertake his work with a new seriousness, feeling that he now had an obligation to fulfill Morcom's potential as well as his own.

Turing would take the entrance exams for Trinity College again in December 1930. Despite his new sense of determination, Turing failed to win the scholarship at Trinity; however, he won an open scholarship to King's College, his second choice. He would enter King's College at Cambridge, and he would fulfill all the plans he had made with Morcom for beginning their two careers. Turing would always hold up Morcom's memory as a challenge—to reach for the highest standard of excellence, at 100 percent effort and more—and to tackle the toughest problems, the ones that could only be solved through great imagination, ingenuity, and insight.

The body by reason of being a living body can 'attract' and hold on to a 'spirit.' [W]hilst the body is alive and awake the two are firmly connected. When the body is asleep I cannot guess what happens but when the body dies the 'mechanism' of the body, holding the spirit is gone and the spirit finds a new body sooner or later, perhaps immediately.

While such ideas might seem to be more the province of religion than of science, they would find an echo in various quantum theories of consciousness that have been proposed since the 1980s, particularly by Roger Penrose, a distinguished British mathematical physicist. Penrose believes that consciousness cannot be explained solely by deterministic processes in physics or chemistry. Penrose asserts that there must also be interaction on the quantum level, with structures called microtubules in brain cells providing the link between conventional and quantum processes. These theories, however, are controversial and not accepted by determinists who believe that all mental phenomena have a physical cause even if that cause cannot yet be shown in detail.

For Turing, Morcom's death seems to have intensified an interest in the nature of thought, the possible relationship between thought and the brain, and even the possibility that someday a machine, too, might also have the mysterious property of intelligence.

The Frontiers
of Mathematics

A lan Turing entered King's College at Cambridge in 1931.
From the beginning, King's College could easily have rated
as Turing's first choice. The school was especially strong in mathematics, Turing's main area of interest, with its faculty including
G. H. Hardy (1877–1947), probably the most prominent British
mathematician; Bertrand Russell (1872–1970), the mathematician
who became even better known as a philosopher; and Max M. H.
Newman (1897–1984), mathematician and later code breaker and
computer pioneer. Other first-rate minds available included John
Maynard Keynes (1883–1946), the influential economist; and E. M.
Forster (1879–1970), the noted novelist and essayist.

Moreover, in the next few years, threatened by the Nazi regime
of Germany and the fascists of Italy, eminent scholars would flee
their homes for freedom and sanctuary in Great Britain and the

Arched gateway at King's College in 1925 (© E. O. Hoppe/CORBIS)

United States. Many of them stopped by Cambridge to give lectures and courses before traveling on, and some of them chose to stay. This wave of flight from the rising tide of totalitarianism brought the mathematics issues of the day right to Turing's doorstep. The graceful towers of one of Britain's two greatest universities (the other being Oxford) gave shelter, and in turn, the students in Turing's class inherited a giant intellectual legacy—from the best of the best of European universities. It was the perfect opportunity to become exposed to cutting-edge science and math.

New Intellectual Opportunities

Moving from the rather rigid and narrow focus of a preparatory school such as Sherborne to one of the world's greatest universities must have both intimidated and thrilled Turing, whose personality combined intellectual brashness with social awkwardness and shyness.

Besides the King's College reputation for strength in math, statistics, economics, and the sciences, King's had also become a magnet for highly creative persons in literary, intellectual, and artistic realms. Many members of the Bloomsbury group (a circle of writers and artists that included Forster, Keynes, and Russell) were associated with or on the faculty there, and as Alan made his way around the campus, and later, when he had dining privileges, he certainly had many opportunities to strike up conversation—but Turing was no more outgoing and social at college than he had been at Sherborne.

Turing's combination of physical awkwardness and energy showed in his athletic efforts, While at King's College, Turing joined the Boat Club—rowing being a popular sport at Cambridge and Oxford. Rowing was a somewhat unusual interest for Turing, since he disliked team sports and generally was not good at them.

On the other hand, Turing loved running, especially by himself and over long distances. He was good—naturally gifted in fact—at this intensely individual sport. He had found himself not only winning in school and interschool competitions at Sherborne, but also, to his surprise, winning respect and applause from his schoolmates who had once picked on him.

Socially, though, the first couple of years were painful, difficult, and lonely for Turing. He did develop feelings for Kenneth Harrison, a fellow science student who reminded him in many ways of Christopher Morcom. As would often happen, Harrison rejected Turing's expression of his desire to go beyond friendship, but they remained friends.

Turing was not a glib conversationalist—he would often stutter as his voice struggled to keep up with his mind. Nevertheless, he was not immune to the political currents that were sweeping through Cambridge and other British universities. With the devastation of the Great War (World War I) fresh in their minds, many students and professors signed pledges to refuse to participate in any future war. Meanwhile, Hitler was consolidating Nazi power in Germany and hungrily eying nearby countries.

A smaller but vocal group went beyond pacifism. They saw German and Italian fascism as an outgrowth of capitalism in general, and for them there was only one real alternative: communism. They looked with hope toward the Soviet Union, where they thought Joseph Stalin was organizing a new kind of society where workers would be treated fairly and there would be no unemployment. (The grim reality of purges and labor camps was largely hidden from them.)

In 1933 Turing wrote:

> *Dear Mother,*
>
> *Thank you for socks etc.* . . . *Am thinking of going to Russia some time in vac[ation] but have not yet quite made up my mind.*
>
> *I have joined an organisation called the 'Anti-War Council.' Politically rather communist. Its programme is principally to organize strikes amongst munitions and chemical workers when government intends to go to war. It gets up a guarantee fund to support the workers who strike* . . .

Fortunately for his work and future career, Turing never went to Russia. While he might have been willing to sign a petition, he was more a liberal or a social democrat than a radical. Besides, politics simply did not interest him in any systematic way. In fact, hardly anything really interested him if it did not involve mathematics or science.

Turing continued to deeply miss Christopher Morcom and the intellectual intimacy they had shared. While he made acquaintances and apparently had his first brief sexual affair with a fellow student named James Atkins, he did not become emotionally involved.

Mathematical Hurdles

The 1930s were important years for science and mathematics at Cambridge. In addition to mathematicians and other scientists already mentioned, the British physicist Paul Dirac (1902–84) had received a Ph.D. in 1926 from Cambridge, going on to become a Fellow the following year and Lucasian Professor in mathematics in 1931. Shortly after the German physicist Werner Heisenberg (1901–76) introduced quantum mechanics at the University of Göttingen, Dirac began work in this exciting new field. Soon Cambridge was Göttingen's close rival.

Another influence on Turing's own scientific thinking would be the astrophysicist Arthur Eddington (1882–1944), who had furnished confirmation of Einstein's theory of relativity. Eddington became a popular writer on the new cosmology and physics, and his belief in the connection between the uncertainty principle in quantum physics and the possibility of free will meshed with Turing's own concerns.

Turing studied under both George Hardy and Eddington, and he soaked up the richness of the school's science culture, thriving on it. He would soon make his mark at King's College. However, it would not come all that easily.

Strangely, when Alan took part 1 of the Tripos (the first part of the final exam) in 1932, his results were embarrassingly poor. As had happened before, at Hazelhurst and Sherborne, he was more concerned about doing well on the more advanced part 2, section A, and the even more challenging and exciting section B (later part 3), even though those exams were still a couple of years away. Now he would have to make up lost points.

"I can hardly look anyone in the face after it . . . ," he wrote to his mother. "I shall just have to get a 1st to shew I'm not really so bad as that."

Not only did Turing do well the next time around, he had by this time caught the attention of John Maynard Keynes and George Hardy. As early as Turing's second year, both had also seen creative potential in the way he had proved a theorem (in logic or mathematics, a provable proposition or formula)—even though the particular theorem had already been proved by someone else. (Turing had continued his habit of just diving into what interested him, instead of researching first to find out whether someone had already obtained the desired result.) Much of the reward in science and math is to gain credit for moving the front line of knowledge. However, in Turing's case, he was so consistently original in his approach to proving theorems and solving problems that he gained credit for the value of his originality and perspective, even though he was not first.

Moreover, in 1934, Turing captured interest for having shown real signs of genius when he looked for a mathematical theory that would explain the bell-shaped curve that turned up in the results of many statistical studies. So, despite duplications, Keynes saw the merit and originality in Turing's work and backed Turing for election to Fellow—a graduate honor that includes a stipend (regular payment), including dining privileges, all without obligations, no teaching or lab assistant chores. All he had to do was choose his topic and just move onto a clear playing field, whatever it was that he chose.

✸ The Scope of Mathematics

Most people never get closer to the subject area of advanced mathematics than using an electronic calculator to pay a bill or running software on their computer to figure the amount of taxes owed. But arithmetic is only one branch of the many-limbed tree that is mathematics.

At the most basic level, math provides tools, rules, and approaches to quantifying substances, liquids, and shapes—measuring, counting, and arranging objects in space. This leads to the slightly more abstract notion of *number.* Numbers abstract quantities and relationships without regard to particular physical objects. After all, $2 + 2 = 4$ whether one is adding apples or stars. The ability to set up equations casting the unknown in terms of the known is the task of algebra, which was first systematically formulated by a Persian/Arab mathematician named Muhammad ibn Mūsā al-Kwārizmī in the ninth century.

In the 17th century, Isaac Newton (1643–1729) and Gottfried von Leibniz (1646–1716) invented calculus, one of the most powerful and essential tools for all the physical sciences. (Roughly speaking, while algebra and geometry deal with fixed relationships, calculus deals with change and the manipulation of infinitesimal quantities.)

By the 18th century, this new form of mathematics had revolutionized physics and astronomy. The 19th century brought some disquieting events, such as the discovery that there were many kinds of infinity and the description of weirdly shaped but fully consistent geometries that did not obey the axioms of Euclid.

The 20th century brought an emphasis on mathematical logic, using mathematics to manipulate mathematics itself. This brought questions of the extent to which mathematics itself was consistent, and whether it was possible to know what was provable. This was the frontier of mathematics that drew Turing's generation, and to which Turing would make a fundamental contribution.

With his own room on campus, Turing had the scholar's ideal circumstances—space, time, and quiet for writing and studying, combined with recognition for the value of his originality and perspective.

Mathematical Logic

Even as the mathematics and physics of the 19th century had achieved an impressive power to explain physical reality, a sort of ghost was discovered in the scientific machine. By the 1930s, quantum theory was talking about uncertainty and the limits of measurement. Physicists now knew that no observation could be made without considering the effects of the observer on what is being measured.

Meanwhile, mathematics had begun to examine its own toolkit—the axioms or assertions that could be used to construct proofs of theorems that could in turn become building blocks for further work.

A new field was emerging, which could be called the mathematics of mathematics. Formally, it was known as mathematical logic, and it dealt with topics such as set theory, the construction and evaluation of formal systems, and the consideration of what could be proven using a given system.

Modern mathematical logic had its roots in the 19th century with the work of logicians such as George Boole (1815–64) and Augustus de Morgan (1806–71). (Boole, in particular, developed the binary logic of AND, OR, and NOT that would later be built into computer circuits and used to formulate today's Web searches.)

In 1910, Bertrand Russell and Alfred North Whitehead (1861–1947) published the first volume of *Principia Mathematica,* an ambitious attempt to create a comprehensive and consistent mathematical logic. However, in 1931, the very year Turing arrived at Cambridge, the German/Austrian mathematician Kurt Gödel (1906–78) proved that there were assertions about numbers that were perfectly legal by the rules of mathematics but could not be proven to be either true or false.

The struggle to determine the ultimate validity of mathematics also had important implications for philosophy (Russell and Whitehead were philosophers as well as mathematicians). Near the end of his time at King's College, Turing would take a class called

Foundations of Mathematics from another philosopher, Ludwig Wittgenstein (1889–1951).

Wittgenstein is often considered to be the founder of modern philosophy. Also called "analytical philosophy," this approach focused on the analysis of propositions, statements, and assertions. Put a bit simplistically, for Wittgenstein a philosophical problem could be recast as a "language problem." If not, it wasn't a valid question at all. In the preface to his massive work, the *Tractatus Logico-Philosophicus*, Wittgenstein says:

> *The whole sense of the book might be summed up in the following words: what can be said at all can be said clearly, and what we cannot talk about we must pass over in silence.*

Indeed, Wittgenstein's philosophy closely paralleled the situation faced by mathematicians. Mathematicians were trying to find a way to determine what kinds of problems could be solved, while the analytical philosophers tried to determine what kinds of questions could be usefully asked.

In the class, Wittgenstein applied his analysis to the terms and concepts used by mathematicians. As quoted by Hodges, for example, Wittgenstein dismisses the famous "Liar paradox" that echoes the kind of mathematical contradictions Hilbert and Russell had been interested in:

> *Think of the case of the Liar. It is very queer in a way that should have puzzled anyone—much more extraordinary than you might think. . . . Because the thing works like this: if a man says, 'I am lying' we say that it follows that he is not lying, from which it follows that he is lying and so on. Well, so what? You can go on like that until you are black in the face. Why not? It doesn't matter. . . . it is just a useless language-game, and why should anyone be excited?*

As the only real mathematician in the class, Turing was often called upon to defend his profession. When Wittgenstein asked why people should be afraid of contradictions inside mathematics, Turing made an interesting reply: "You cannot be confident about applying your calculus until you know there is no hidden contradiction to it." Turing, whose interest included aspects of the natural sciences and even engineering, was pointing out that contradictions in our understanding of the world could have real consequences: "Although you do not know that the bridge will fall if there are no contradictions, yet it is almost certain that if there are contradictions it will go wrong somewhere."

Hilbert's Challenge

It so happened one day when Turing was attending one of the foundation lectures that the name David Hilbert came up. Hilbert (1862–1943), a brilliant German mathematician, had the kind of energy and focus that the new mathematics needed. At 38, he churned up the 1900 meeting of the International Congress of Mathematicians in Paris with a list of 23 major problems that he challenged his colleagues to solve. These problems, Hilbert emphasized, needed to be resolved if mathematics was to move forward into the realms of logic and beyond the use of numbers just for counting, measuring, and other applied purposes. It was an important moment in the history of mathematics. Hilbert had thrown down the gauntlet, serving the challenge—and in the coming decades this challenge showed mathematicians rising to the occasion.

Then, nearly three decades later, in 1928, Hilbert came back again with list in hand, this time to renew the challenge for problems still unresolved from his original list, plus a few new ones.

In the spring of 1935, Turing attended a course given by Max Newman—a course that may have changed Turing's entire life focus.

During a class lecture Turing attended, one of Hilbert's challenges caught his interest. This is called the Decision Problem (or, in German, *Entscheidungsproblem*) and it went like this: For any properly constructed mathematical assertion, is there a step-by-step method (an algorithm) that can determine whether the assertion is provable?

At least since the time of Leibniz, scientists had pursued the answer to the decision problem. In the late 1600s, Gottfried Leibniz had hoped for the possibility of having a calculus of reason that one could engage to solve all disagreements quickly, surely, automatically, and accurately. Or, to put the matter another way, how smoothly the world could be run if one just knew, given a few solid premises and a reasonable-sounding conclusion, if one could be sure that the problem had "computability," as Turing called it, so that one could just know that in due time one would obtain a definite, accurate, and defensible answer. Or, if not—if one just knew in advance that the matter at hand could *not* be resolved with a computation—then no time need be further wasted on trying to find the computation.

That was the decision problem. Are there some problems that do not lend themselves to computational resolutions? Does the usefulness of computation have

David Hilbert challenged 20th-century mathematicians by posing 23 problems that he said needed to be solved. (AIP Emilio Segrè Visual Archives, Lande Collection)

limits? As Jim Holt says, writing for the *New Yorker* on this subject: "The decision problem calls for a mechanical set of rules for deciding whether an inference is valid, one that is guaranteed to yield a yes-or-no answer in a finite amount of time." Hilbert called it "the principal problem of mathematical logic."

Turing could not have known that the way he would choose to tackle this problem would help win a world war and lead to the computer revolution that has reshaped today's world.

Calculating Minds

Sometimes in the history of science or mathematics, a breakthrough is the result not of someone thinking harder about a problem but thinking *differently* about it. This was the case of Turing. He would tackle the decision problem essentially by translating it into an equivalent problem, that of computability.

The computability problem can be stated like this: Given an *algorithm*, or step-by-step procedure for solving a numeric problem, can it be shown that the procedure will work for any appropriate numbers fed into it?

For example, the question "given two numbers x and y, does y evenly divide into x?" can be easily resolved simply by performing the division and seeing if there is a remainder.

A harder problem is determining whether a given number is prime—that is, divisible only by itself and 1. There are a variety of algorithms for finding prime numbers. The simplest one is to divide the given number by every number from 2 up to the half of the number and see if it ever divides evenly. If it doesn't, the number is prime. There are certainly faster algorithms, but as the potential prime numbers get bigger the amount of computation required goes up rapidly. Nevertheless, the algorithm always works in theory.

Turing's key insight was that Hilbert's question about provability was mathematically equivalent to that of computability. And any properly constructed set of computing instructions should, in theory, be able to be carried out by a machine—a computer.

From Abacus to Calculator

Mechanical computing has a surprisingly long history. Archaeologists have found evidence that a calculating device—a forerunner of the abacus—was invented about 4,000 years before the Christian era (4000 B.C.E.). Probably invented in its early forms by the Babylonians, a later, hand-held version of the abacus developed by the Romans was widely used by engineers to calculate viaducts, roads, and land surveys; by tradespeople as cash registers, calculators, and computers; and, probably by tax collectors to figure the amounts due. Eventually, the abacus was used throughout the Near East as well as China.

The abacus is a digital computer in that it works with discrete quantities (one bead is equal to one, 10, 100, and so on, depending on its position.) The other kind of computer is an analog computer—a computing device that operates on measurable quantities (for example, weight or length) rather than having direct numerical input (and sometimes output). An analog clock is one example

The oldest known analog "computer" is a mysterious machine found in 1901 among the strewn cargo of an ancient shipwreck at the bottom of the Aegean Sea. Dubbed the Antikythera device, it apparently dates from the first century B.C.E., and as far as anyone knows, this calculating machine stands alone in its time—with not even a mention of anything like it in any ancient document. Nothing similar from the same era has ever been found. Was it a one-of-a-kind production?

Both types of computers were further developed in the Middle Ages and Renaissance periods. In analog computing, Near Eastern astronomers developed the astrolabe and other instruments for measuring star positions.

Babbage, Lovelace, and Their "Difference Engine"

The most remarkable forerunner of the modern computer came in the middle of the 19th century, though its significance would not be realized until well into Turing's time.

Charles Babbage (1791–1871) was an ingenious British inventor and mathematician. Born in Devonshire, he attended the University of Cambridge, and in 1816, he became a Fellow of the Royal Society—a great honor, especially at the age of 24. Along with a group of friends including astronomer John Herschel, Babbage helped establish the Analytical Society in 1812. He was also a founding member of the Royal Astronomical Society (1820), and helped form the Statistical Society (1834).

Babbage became frustrated by the inaccuracy of the hand-compiled tables of logarithms and other quantities that were available of the time. He decided that only a machine that could follow precise, unvarying steps could guarantee the accuracy of calculations. In this era of locomotives and steam-driven looms, it was perhaps not surprising that Babbage thought it quite possible to build a "Difference Engine" to perform complicated calculations quickly and automatically.

Meanwhile, Ada Byron (1815–52), countess of Lovelace and daughter of the British poet Lord Byron, had grown up having an innate interest in mathematics. Self-taught in geometry, she also learned by whatever other means were available to her, including friends, tutors, and classes in astronomy and math. She and Babbage met in 1833 (when she was about 18) and these two individuals with a passion for numbers began collaborating.

Like Jacquard's loom with its punched-card weaving patterns, the Difference Engine relied on programming concepts and had a complex design capable of handling extensive and involved calculations. Lovelace showed a ready understanding of the concept of a programmed machine when she translated and annotated a paper

In the 1650s, the English mathematician William Oughtred (1575–1660) invented the slide rule, using a stick marked with logarithmic measurements that slid up and down to deliver the results. After various improvements through the years, the slide rule

written in French about Babbage's Difference Engine. Money for the project ran out, though, and Babbage and Lovelace never saw it work. However, in 1991 a team of computer experts carefully followed Babbage's design notes and drawings and found that the design was sound and the Babbage Difference Engine they produced ran perfectly.

Lovelace and Babbage also collaborated on designing a more advanced machine—the Analytical Engine, which is considered the first attempt at a modern digital computer. The machine was designed to read data from a stack of punched cards—much as early digital computers did—and it could store the data and perform calculations. Byron worked on writing the instructions, or programming, recorded by punching the cards—and she therefore receives recognition as the first computer programmer. In 1979, in honor of the contributions to computer science made by Lady Ada Lovelace, the U.S. Department of Defense named a key programming language Ada.

The Analytical Engine probably would not have been a very practical machine, however, even if the thousands of precisely machined parts had been manufactured and assembled. These early computer designers had not come up with the idea of using the same format and media for all functions—programming, data storage, results. Electricity and electronics were not yet in the picture, and the calculating circuits made possible by Boolean logic were as yet unknown.

By the 1930s, however, electrical switches and relays as well as the much faster electronic vacuum tubes were readily available. A number of people in the United States, Great Britain, and Germany had begun to build electrical or electronic calculators. What was needed were the ideas to put it all together—the universal, programmable computer. Alan Turing's work would play a key—perhaps the most decisive—role in this development.

became a staple instrument for every engineer and scientist well into the 20th century, tucked away in a desk drawer or handy pocket for quick calculations. Finally, in the 1970s handheld calculators replaced them, especially as the microchip-driven pocket calculator became more and more sophisticated.

Mechanical Calculators

Mechanical digital calculators also advanced in the 17th century. The German scholar and inventor Wilhelm Schickard (1592–1635) built the first successful cogs-and-wheels calculating machine. He described it in a letter to the famous astronomer Johannes Kepler (1571–1630):

> *What you have done by calculation I have just tried to do by way of mechanics. I have conceived a machine consisting of eleven complete and six incomplete sprocket wheels; it calculates instantaneously and automatically from given numbers, as it adds, subtracts, multiplies, and divides. You would enjoy to see how the machine accumulates and transports spontaneously a ten or a hundred to the left and, vice-versa, how it does the opposite if it is subtracting. . . .*

Schickard was followed by the French mathematician Blaise Pascal (1623–62) and by the German Gottfried Wilhelm von Leibniz, who built their own calculators. (Leibniz in particular was enthusiastic about computing, asserting that "It is unworthy of excellent men to lose hours like slaves in the labor of calculation which could safely be relegated to anyone else if machines were used."

As the 1930s drew to an end, the components of modern computing were slipping into place: mathematical logic (including Boolean algebra), together with electrical and electronic circuits. Also on tap was the punch-card data processing technology first developed in the late 19th century by the American inventor Herman Hollerith (1860–1929).

There was a growing realization that the complexity of modern industry and communications and the need of governments and business to collect and process statistical data was outstripping the capacity of mechanical devices (such as tabulators), even in the hands of skilled operators. What was needed was a means of rapid automatic computation, where a set of instructions could be repeatedly applied without human intervention. This would require both a conceptual breakthrough and a technological advance. For that,

Boole's Bridge to the Computer

One of the missing pieces of the computing puzzle of the 1930s was how to connect the logic of mathematics to the physical operation of an automatic computing machine. Turing and later computer designers found an answer in the work of a 19th-century logician, George Boole.

As a young student, George did not at first take to math, preferring the classics, but began investigating math when he was about 17. Most of his learning was self-taught, but he started out as assistant master of a school in South Yorkshire in northern England at 16. His knack for teaching and breadth of learning made a place for him in other schools. Finally, Boole showed himself to be so plainly qualified intellectually that, despite his lack of formal training, he was awarded the position of professor of mathematics at Queen's College, Cork (later University College Cork) in Ireland.

George Boole wrote "Investigation of the Laws of Thought," a treatise published in 1854 on what is now known as Boolean algebra. He contended that logic, which had generally been taught as a form of philosophy, is actually closer to mathematics. Whereas arithmetic uses the basic functions of division, multiplication, addition, and subtraction, Boolean algebra uses similar operators including "AND," "OR," and "NOT." Also, parallel to geometry, Boolean algebra is based on a handful of basic axioms. What Turing and others were realizing by the mid 1930s was that the binary (true/false) values of Boolean logic and its simple but powerful operations could be represented directly by the physical position of a switch or relay or the activation of a vacuum tube. Storing numbers in binary (base two) rather than the customary decimal format made it easy to apply logical operations to them. In turn, the logical operations could be used to perform calculations such as multiplication.

though, mathematicians would have to take an interest in the details of computation.

The Turing Machine

If one were to ask a mathematician of the early 1930s what computing machines might have to do with mathematics, the response would likely be puzzlement. Adding machines or desktop tabulators might be able to do arithmetic, but that would be of little interest to the pure mathematician.

Thus, most mathematicians looking at the Decision Problem posed by Hilbert would have approached it as a traditional proof using the notation of symbolic logic. Probably, they would have considered attempting an extension of Kurt Gödel's work. Gödel had developed an ingenious way to "do mathematics with mathematics" by assigning unique numbers to the various formal statements or "sentences" that can be formulated in a mathematical system. He then showed that a complete system (which accounts for all relevant theory) cannot be consistent; a consistent theory cannot be complete.

The question of whether a given statement was computable could be addressed by creating a "symbolic calculus" that would allow mathematical statements to be manipulated and evaluated. An analogy might be to use rules of grammar to analyze the form of a question to determine whether it was answerable.

Rather than working on the symbolic level, however, Turing hit upon a completely original approach to the decision problem. First, he showed that the decision problem was equivalent to the problem of determining whether a given mathematical function could be definitively calculated—that it was computable. A mathematical function is essentially a statement of relationship between input and output. For example, the value of the function $f(x) = 2x$ for any value x would be double that value. Thus if $x = 4$, $f(x) = 8$.

Turing then defined computability in terms of the ability to apply a series of specified steps—an algorithm. If an algorithm could be shown to always provide a definite result for any value put into the function, then that function is computable.

Next, Turing needed a mechanical method for applying an algorithm by combining a set of simple operations. This, of course, is what computers do today—but there were no general-purpose digital computers at the time.

Instead, Turing created a computer in his mind. He visualized a continuous roll of square paper sections. (One might visualize an endless strip of toilet paper or paper towels.) He asked himself what he needed when he sat down to solve a calculation—a pad of paper, a pencil, and instructions that break the process down to the simplest possible steps. He wanted just the essence of the process. When he had eliminated all but the most necessary elements of the machine, all he had really was the infinite strip of toilet paper, a little scanner to determine the contents of a given square, and the following operations:

- the ability to write one of a specified set of symbols on the current square (in the most common Turing machine, there are two symbols, 1 and 0, where 0 is equivalent to "blank")
- the ability to erase the current square (which is the same as saying replacing its symbol with the symbol "blank")
- the ability to move the tape one square to the left or right, thereby changing the position of the machine's "head" or pointer
- a register in which the machine can store its current "state"—essentially a label that describes what the machine has just done.

The other necessary component was an instruction table that tells the machine what operation to perform when it sees a given symbol (or a blank) in the current square and the machine is in a given state.

The beginning of an instruction table might look like this:

Current State	Scanned Symbol	Print Symbol	Move Tape	New State
A	0	1	R	B
A	1	1	L	C
B	0	1	L	A

In this example, the machine starts out in state A. If the current square has a 0 (blank), it prints a 1 and then moves the tape one space to the right. It then changes the state to B. If, however, the current square had a 1, the machine leaves the 1 unchanged and moves the tape one square to the left, changing the current state to C.

The machine then repeats the process: Scan the current square, execute the printing and movement instructions according to the current state, and then change the state as specified.

Turing could use this imaginary little machine to get at a lot of answers about logic and mathematics. People began to call this kind of virtual machine a "Turing machine," or, sometimes, a "paper machine." They were small and they were simple, but Turing could get some very complex problem solving out of them. He tried the vexing paradoxes that haunt logicians, such as: "I am lying." "There

The Power of Simplicity

In tackling the Decision Problem, Turing applied one of the most powerful tools available to any problem solver—simplification. That is, find the essence of the problem by getting rid of anything extraneous. Thus, Turing worked on building an abstract version of his machine—a machine of the mind. He pared down the complexities, minimizing to the absolute essence of the machine he needed. It would be, simply, his concept of a machine that could answer Hilbert's question.

The typewriter came closest among existing machines. Yet the typewriter was not quite right in several ways. It needed a human operator to put each letter, one by one, in a single line across the page. Turing's machine had to be automated. Turing also dispensed with the unneeded features of the typewriter, such as the ability to move the carriage to the next line.

When he was finished simplifying, the details fell in place, and he could use his vision of the essential tool for the job. Creating this kind of thought experiment created a bridge between the physical and the putative worlds—and kept one's thinking on track.

is only one untrue statement on this page" (and the only thing on the page is the statement).

To attack the decision problem, Turing showed that the input and output of a mathematical function was equivalent to the input and output of what we would now call a computer program. Any program that can process data can also process a program as though it were data. The question of computability is then equivalent to the question of whether a computer program will ever successfully compute a result and halt. Using his imaginary machine, Turing showed that there was no guarantee that, given a program and input to that program, one could determine whether the program will eventually halt (other than running the program and waiting for an indefinite amount of time.)

In the end, Turing could thus prove that there were mathematical assertions whose results could not be determined. This was

Some historians suggest that this aspect of Turing's thought processes—this bridge-building between the tactile, physical world and the world of the mind—was one of Turing's greatest gifts to mathematics and the key that opened up the world of computers.

Turing's physical intuition resembled that of another famously eccentric and highly creative scientist, the American physicist Richard Feynman (1918–88). Turing and the MIT (later Caltech) physicist were contemporaries, though separated by the Atlantic. As far as we know, they never met.

Like Turing, Feynman had a very complicated problem to solve: the quantum dynamics of the electron (the particle first named by Turing's distant relation George Johnstone Stoney.) And like Turing, Feynman was able to grasp the problem by visualizing it in its simplest terms. As a result, Feynman showed that what had appeared to be an infinitely complex problem could be tackled through a series of manageable computations. Feynman then devised a system of diagrams to aid in each step in the series, thus making quantum mechanics far more accessible to succeeding generations of students.

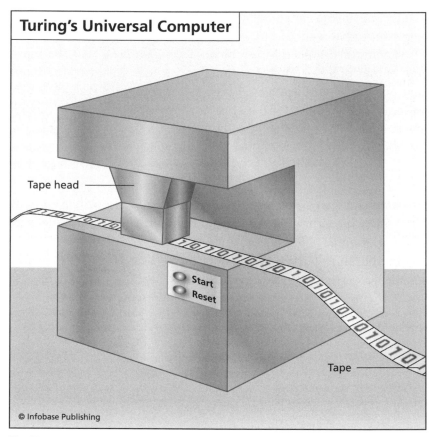

Turing's Universal Computer

Tape head

Start
Reset

Tape

© Infobase Publishing

The Turing machine was a "paper computer" that in principle would calculate anything that would be computed.

equivalent to showing that the Decision Problem posed by Hilbert could not be solved.

A Universal Machine

If a Turing machine could be used only to solve the decision problem or other problems in mathematical logic, it would still have been an important milestone in mathematics. However, the Turing machine has another important characteristic: It is a universal machine. Turing showed that his machine would compute anything that *could* be computed. True, there are problems that the device might take an infinite amount of time to compute, but that was a matter of engineering. Computers, as just about everyone knows, get faster and more powerful every few years, making more applications practicable.

At 23, Alan Turing had solved one of David Hilbert's list of problems. However, he had barely begun preparing to submit his paper for publication when a paper arrived at Cambridge from Princeton University across the Atlantic. The American mathematician and logician Alonzo Church (1903–95) at Princeton had also solved the Decision Problem (using the more symbolic approach mentioned earlier) and he had (alas) already published his results. Turing's adviser Max Newman wrote Church and suggested that he help Turing come to Princeton as a graduate student and supervise his work for the doctorate.

Church accepted the request and also agreed to evaluate or "referee" Turing's paper for publication. (Indeed, Church was probably the only mathematician who had sufficient background in the new theory of computability to take on that task.)

As a result of this collaboration, something exceptional happened. Normally in mathematics and science, only the first person to publish a new result gets the credit. In this case, however, because Turing's way of attacking the Decision Problem was so original and had so many implications for computational theory, Turing received full credit for what became known as the Church-Turing Thesis.

Graduate Study at Princeton

Turing's first impressions of America and Americans were not favorable. Sailing on the ocean liner to America, Turing wrote to his mother:

> It strikes me that Americans can be the most insufferable and insensitive creatures you could wish. One of them has just been talking to me and telling me of the worst aspects of America with evident pride. However they may not all be like that.

Of course, Turing was hardly a man of the world and had little experience of other cultures.

John von Neumann made fundamental contributions to computing, game theory, quantum physics, and other fields. (AIP Emilio Segrè Visual Archives)

Turing's first sight of Princeton University, with its architecture modeled after Cambridge and Oxford, must at least have looked comforting. Turing also discovered that the American university had modeled much of its social life and customs after the older British institutions.

In 1932, a generous bequest had led to the formation of the Institute for Advanced Study at Princeton. The new institution had quickly attracted some of the world's best mathematicians and physicists, including many who had fled from the ominous Nazi power in Germany. Besides Church, of course, Turing could meet Albert Einstein and consult with G. H. Hardy (who had settled there earlier) as well as the multitalented and charismatic Hungarian-American mathematician John von Neumann (1903–57).

Some historians point out that von Neumann is frequently credited with innovations in computing that were actually Turing's, and that may be true, but von Neumann also was the only person at Princeton who seemed to recognize Turing's true stature. He pointed out that Turing had introduced a completely new topic to consider—"computability." Von Neumann was smooth and confident in social situations, used as he was to Viennese sophisticates, and his manners and presence were nothing like Turing's, but he did show a great appreciation for Turing's intellect.

Turing extended and strengthened his work on computable numbers and its connection to Church's equivalent "lambda calculus." The result was the dissertation that won him his doctorate in June 1938.

For all his mathematical opportunities, Turing was not very happy in New Jersey. While he did participate in some social activities (and even joined in impromptu hockey matches against the women students at Vassar College), Turing continued to be dissatisfied with his social possibilities. (Not surprisingly, while he had accepted his homosexuality as a reality, he still lacked the combination of boldness and subterfuge that would be needed to navigate

Henry Burchard Fine Hall at Princeton University, housing the Department of Mathematics (Princeton University Archives, Department of Rare Books and Special Collections)

the highly closeted gay world of even a rather liberal institution like Princeton in the 1930s.)

Even ordinary conversation often irritated Turing. He did not understand American slang and the tendency of Princeton intellectuals to make small talk and avoid discussing their work in earnest. Thus, Turing spent much of his time alone. Von Neumann, meanwhile, was so impressed with Turing that he offered the younger man a job as his assistant. However, Turing turned him down and headed home to Cambridge in 1938.

In Turing's baggage was a bit of computer hardware he had constructed. It was an electromechanical calculator that used Boolean logic "gates" and other circuits, and it could multiply two binary numbers (consisting of 1s and 0s) together. The device represented the first concrete step toward making the universal Turing machine a physical reality.

On Turing's mind was a practical application for the new mechanical mathematical logic. In a letter to his mother, Turing wrote:

> *You have often asked me about possible applications of various branches of mathematics. I have just discovered a possible application of the kind of thing I am working on at present. It answers the question "What is the most general kind of code or cypher possible," and at the same time (rather naturally) enables me to construct a lot of particular and interesting codes.*

Turing could scarcely have known that soon he would be called on to spearhead history's greatest code-breaking effort.

Enigma

Most young people have been fascinated by secret codes and ciphers, and Alan Turing was no exception. (Roughly, *codes* work at the word level; *ciphers* work letter by letter.) At Sherborne, Turing and his friend Chris Morcom enjoyed creating and deciphering messages written and read using their own, intricate codes. The two boys especially liked a system that used a template—carefully cut in a specific pattern so that when the template was placed over a particular portion of the text—on a specific page, in a specific book—the message was revealed.

By the 1930s, codes and ciphers were so intriguing to that generation of youngsters that manufacturers of dry cereal and similar products marketed their wares by including "decoder rings" and other gizmos to encourage purchases. The subjects of secret agents, cryptograms, codes, and ciphers were popular in comic books and on the movie screen. With a decoder ring, a kid could pretend to be receiving a secret message from the likes of Buck Rogers, the Green Hornet, or Batman.

Increasingly, though, codes and ciphers were a serious real-world business. World War I had brought the first widespread use of radio for coordinating military activity, along with the use of ciphers to encrypt radio traffic. The new communications technology brought the need to analyze the communications traffic of enemy nations and, with luck, to "break" ciphers to reveal the message contents.

In 1914, the British Admiralty (navy department) established the code-breaking operation that became known as Room 40. Only a few hours after war had been declared, Room 40 had its greatest triumph. The crew of a British undersea cable-laying ship cut into the cable carrying German telegraph traffic. After decrypting one message, they discovered that it contained instructions to the German embassy in Mexico that in the event of Germany becoming involved in war with the United States, Mexico would be offered the states of Texas, New Mexico, and Arizona in return for an alliance with Germany. The British promptly forwarded the cable to American authorities. The resulting uproar infuriated the American public and helped turn the Americans toward supporting Britain and its allies, though the United States did not actually enter the war until 1917.

Despite the considerable importance of cryptography in the new ways of war, traditionalists in both the United States and Britain were not comfortable with what was viewed as a sneaky and underhanded way of fighting. Indeed, in 1929 the U.S. secretary of state ordered the closing of a cryptanalytic (code-breaking) office, saying, "Gentlemen don't read each other's mail."

By the 1930s, however, it was clear that securing one's own communications while successfully cracking the opponent's ciphers would be vital in any future war—a war of far-flung armies that would be fought in the air and under the sea as well as on land. In this new, highly mobile and fluid kind of war, forces could be assembled and brought to bear in a matter of a few days, not the weeks and months needed in former wars. Determining the enemy's strength and intentions as quickly as possible was vital, and this meant intercepting, decrypting, and understanding the opponent's communications.

By the late 1930s, the British had begun to recruit people who showed talent for cryptology, and mathematicians, naturally, were high on that list. After all, breaking codes required being able to discern subtle patterns or inconsistencies in the text, and mathematics was all about the analysis and manipulation of patterns. Meanwhile, as Hitler continued to make belligerent threats against Germany's neighbors, Turing had begun thinking more realistically about deciphering enemy codes in the event of war. Even while Turing was still studying math at King John's College, he volunteered to receive training from the Government Code and Cypher School (G.C.&C.S.), the successor to the previous war's Room 40.

The German Enigma

After World War I, the German inventor/engineer Arthur Scherbius (1878–1929) came up with a new idea for high-security top-secret communications. It was an intriguing cipher machine, which he called by the name Enigma, a word meaning a mystery or riddle. The machine was first publicized in 1923 at the congress of the Universal Postal Union.

Although three other inventors had designed similar machines independently—one each in the United States, the Netherlands, and Norway—the Enigma proved to be a superior design, and some commercial sales of the Enigma had already taken place to large businesses. However, Scherbius knew his best potential customer for the Enigma would be the Imperial German Navy, which needed secure radio communications for its fleets. Therefore, he wrote to the German navy about his machine, noting in his letter that he thought his cipher machine had several significant advantages. For example, Scherbius pointed out that the Enigma was so designed that its operation "would avoid any repetition of the sequence of letters when the same letter is struck millions of times." In effect, the Enigma would not be a single cipher, but a means to generate a continuous series of ever-changing patterns.

Scherbius also claimed that the "solution of a telegram is also impossible if a machine falls into unauthorized hands, since it requires a prearranged key system."

A German U-boat, probably a U-47, returning to Kiel, Germany, from a war patrol, photographed from or near the battleship Scharnhorst in late 1939 or early 1940. Secure communications were particularly important for submarines, which operated independently for months at a time. (U.S. Naval Historical Center Photograph)

Surprisingly, the German navy did not immediately show interest, nor did the diplomatic branch of the government, which Scherbius also thought would be a naturally strong customer. Finally, though, the navy did agree to buy the Enigma after some new security features were added for military use. Germany also bought the Enigma for use in diplomacy, as well as in other branches of government.

A Fiendishly Complicated Machine

In its simplest form, a cipher is a system where a message (called *plaintext*) is turned into a coded message (or *ciphertext*) by substituting a different letter for each letter in the message. For example, if each letter were replaced with the next letter in the alphabet, the word *war* would be encoded as "xbs." A simple cipher like this would be very easy to guess, so in practice the ciphering systems in use by the early 20th century had more complicated rules or made a repeated series of substitutions.

The Enigma created a very complex mechanical cipher. To send a message, the operator first set three (later four) wheels called rotors so that the letters for that day's general code key showed in the window. Next, another code or "indicator" different for each message was used to encode the daily code key, which would appear at the start of the ciphertext message. Finally, to scramble messages even

German Enigma machine: The German sign translates to "Attention!" (National Security Agency)

more, the operator of a military Enigma also made specified connections in a plug board on the front of the machine.

The operator was now ready to create the encrypted message. When the operator typed a letter of the plaintext, a light would illuminate the corresponding letter of ciphertext. Unlike the case with a simple cipher, however, the same letter would not be encoded the same way each time. Instead, the rotors moved, creating a continuously changing cipher system.

The person receiving an Enigma encrypted message would reverse the process. First, insert the rotors needed for that day's messages, set them to the general settings for the day, and make the plug

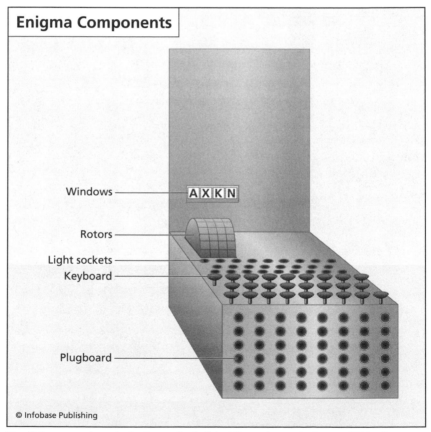

The Enigma may have looked complicated, but the real complexity was hidden in mazes of wiring.

board settings specified for that day. Next, decode the message key (at the beginning of the message), and use it to set the rotors for that message. Finally, type the characters of the encrypted message on the Enigma's keyboard, noting which letter lights up each time. The transcribed message (which would be in German, of course) would be the original plaintext.

Because of its use of three rotors that could be selected from five possibilities, the movable notched rings around the rotors, and the plug board, the Enigma machine had trillions of possible settings. This is why the Germans believed that their code machine was unbreakable. However, encrypting and decoding Enigma messages was rather tedious, and operators often used shortcuts. It would be mainly human failings rather than mechanical flaws that would compromise the Enigma's vaunted security.

The First Assault on the Enigma

In 1932, French agents obtained an instruction manual for Enigma machine operators. They gave a copy to the Polish secret service. The Poles, whose fragile independence could be threatened at any time by their far more powerful neighbor Germany, badly wanted the ability to read German radio traffic. They put three mathematicians to work figuring out from the instructions how the Enigma rotors must be wired. Further, the instructions gave all the information needed to encode two months' worth of messages except for the rotor positions. This went a long way to figuring out the details of the circuits.

To decode an Enigma message, the receiving operator had to know how to set the rotors to match the position used by the sender. Thus, the rotor positions had to be sent using a separate cipher key (usually printed in a special code book). The Polish mathematicians were able to decode these rotor specifications, aided in part by the fact that (at the time) the Germans always repeated them twice to guard against garbled transmissions. Until 1938, therefore, the Poles, French, and other likely enemies of Germany had the ability to break German Enigma codes.

In 1938, the Germans introduced a more complicated system that was harder to decode. However, there were still some patterns

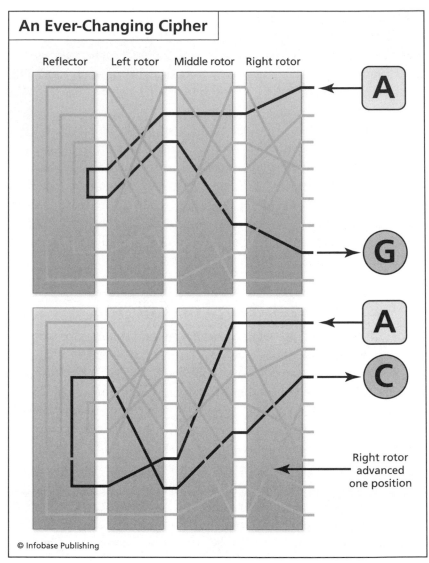

An Ever-Changing Cipher

Reflector   Left rotor   Middle rotor   Right rotor

A

G

A

C

Right rotor
advanced
one position

© Infobase Publishing

The wiring and stepping motion of the Enigma rotors guaranteed that the same letter would be encrypted differently each time it was typed.

that could be used by code breakers. For example, the Enigma was designed so that no letter could be encoded as itself—that is, an *a* in the plaintext would never appear as an *a* in the ciphertext. Further, the fact that the same phrases (such as "weather report" or even "Heil Hitler") appeared in many messages on the same day also made it possible to guess what some words might be and use them in turn to find further patterns. (Such likely phrases were called cribs, because like a student's hidden notes, they could help them "cheat" in solving the cipher.)

The goal was to find the rotor settings that were used to encode a group of messages. Do that, and any other messages for that day could be decoded simply by setting up one's own Enigma machine (or a reverse-engineered copy). The problem was finding which of many thousands of possible rotor settings compatible with a partially guessed cipher was actually the correct one.

The Poles came up with a clever solution: They built a machine that consisted essentially of a bunch of Enigma rotor assemblies, wired together so they could quickly step through the rotor positions and look for key patterns. They called the machine a Bombe—many commentators believe that the name came from the ticking sound the machine made while it was running.

Aided by the Bombe, the Poles continued to decrypt the Enigma messages. Unfortunately, the Germans then added a new wrinkle to their Enigma. Now Enigma operators would select three of a total of five rotors to use in the machine on a given day. Instead of six possible combinations of three rotors ($1 \times 2 \times 3$) there were 60 ($5 \times 4 \times 3$) possibilities. It looked like decoding them would require a Bombe with 60 rotors—too many to be practicable.

Turing and Bletchley Park

On September 1, 1939, Germany launched an invasion of Poland. In accordance with their mutual defense treaties, Britain and France went to war against Germany two days later. The next day, Turing arrived at a place known as Bletchley Park—a pleasant Victorian mansion with a view of the valley below, having low, rolling hills, spacious lawns, and the look of a gentleman farmer's summer home, which it once had been. Turing and others were billeted at hotels in the nearby village of Bletchley, usually dully quiet. Not so, during these days, though, as organizations moved 17,000 children away from London to the relative safety of the regions around Bletchley. (Conveniently, Bletchley was located on the railroad line between the great universities of Oxford and Cambridge, providing ready access to the many academics being enlisted as code breakers.)

The people selected to work at Bletchley Park were quite a diverse lot. They included mathematicians and linguists, but also people who demonstrated a skill for pattern recognition in other fields, such as chess masters and people who liked to solve tough crossword puzzles. Eventually, the core group of code-breaking experts would number about 60. They would be supported by others who had the job of intercepting, classifying, and transcribing the radio transmissions being picked up by a network of 10 listening posts.

Meanwhile, some villagers, not knowing what was going on at Bletchley, complained that these young men at work in the comely

The Battle of the Atlantic

Why did the British spend so much money and send so many people to Bletchley Park to break the German ciphers? The most important reason was this: They desperately needed to win one of history's most unusual battles: the Battle of the Atlantic. The battleground was thousands of square miles of ocean. On one side were the cargo ships that brought desperately needed food, fuel, munitions, and other supplies to a besieged Britain. On the other side, sleek, deadly German submarines (U-boats), often traveling in hunting groups called wolf packs.

For protection, the cargo ships traveled in groups called convoys, guarded by destroyers and other escort ships. While the warships could chase the subs and attack them with depth charges, the first warning of a U-boat attack was often a huge explosion as a torpedo "broke the back" of a ship and sank it.

Throughout the war, the Allies and Germans developed weapons designed to give their side an advantage in the battle on and under the waves. The Allies would develop better radar and sound detection (sonar) to detect subs, more effective depth charge launchers, and eventually, escort carriers with antisubmarine aircraft. The Germans would counter with improved submarines, the snorkel (which enabled subs to stay underwater while they recharged their batteries), and acoustic homing torpedoes.

mansion were not "doing their part," for the war effort. Even the local member of Parliament nearly got into the fray. Generally, though, with so much commotion over the children being settled around the countryside, the employees of GC&CS and their comings and goings did not gain much attention. There was, however, one boy who remarked loudly, "I'll read your secret writing, mister." The incident was slightly unsettling.

As usual, Turing settled in after his own fashion without paying much attention to appearances. He unassumingly rode his bike to the house on the hill and sometimes helped tend bar at his hotel in the evenings. However, there was no doubt that he stood out even in a group that included more than its share of eccentric people. Based

---

The best defense against the wolf packs was to know where they would be operating in time to route convoys around them. Planes could also bomb and harass the subs if they could find them. The most effective way to find subs was to intercept the radio messages being sent between the wolf packs and the German submarine bases—and those messages were encrypted using the particularly tough Naval Enigma cipher.

The German objective was simple: Sink cargo ships faster than the Americans and British could build them, and the supply lines to the island nation of Britain would be cut, crippling industry and threatening starvation. For a while, it looked like Germany might achieve that result, but the combination of radar, improved weapons, and particularly the ability to read the orders the Germans were sending to their subs would prove to be decisive by mid-1943.

Having won the Battle of the Atlantic, the Allies could stockpile supplies and build the invasion force of Americans, British, and Canadians who would land in Normandy, France, in June 1944. Meanwhile, they could also ship many tons of supplies to help the Soviet Union in its own battle against the millions of German soldiers who had invaded Russia.

Thus, by playing a key role in winning the Battle of the Atlantic, Turing and the other code breakers at Bletchley Park could justly claim to have contributed decisively to the Allied victory in World War II.

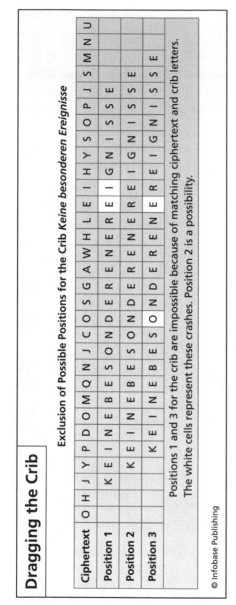

By finding places where ciphertext and suspected plaintext match, cryptanalysts could narrow the range of possible locations.

on interviews with people who knew Turing, the cryptography historian David Kahn wrote:

Turing was a prodigy, a genius. A tallish, dark-haired, powerfully built man with sunken cheeks and deep-set blue eyes, he wore unpressed clothes and picked at the flesh around his fingernails until it bled, stammered, fell into long silences, rarely made eye contact, sidled through doorways, ran long distance races and had, by the time he arrived at B.D., made two fundamental contributions to knowledge.

New Code-breaking Techniques

After war had broken out and the British were given the results of the Polish research, they were dismayed. Even if they could somehow build a big enough mechanical Bombe-type machine, the Germans could render it worthless just by introducing additional rotors for operators to choose from. They needed to find ways to drastically reduce the

A Wave (woman naval volunteer) working with a "Bombe" code-breaking machine (National Security Agency)

number of possible key settings (rotor and plug board positions) that needed to be checked against a given Enigma message.

To do this, the code breakers would seek to exploit both weaknesses in the Enigma system and carelessness on the part of its operators. Each of the millions of initial Enigma machine settings had its own internal consistency. The fact that at a given step a certain letter is encoded as a particular second letter meant that other possible letter matchings could not occur. It was thus possible to winnow away many possible settings.

Turing and his colleagues also refined the techniques for looking for "cribs"—common phrases like "nothing special to report." Because an Enigma cannot encrypt a letter as itself, if that letter is in a crib, the crib could be matched against the ciphertext. Any position where a crib letter matched a cipher letter was a place where the crib could not have been in the plaintext.

Other techniques took advantage of cyclical patterns in the operation of the rotors, caused by the pawls or notches with which an outer rotor could step an inner rotor one position forward. These patterns could be punched onto cards that could be aligned for easier comparison.

The result of all these techniques (and more) was to whittle millions of possible rotor settings down to a hundred thousand or so—a number that could be feasibly examined by a Bombe.

In general, Turing's mind in particular was well prepared for the mixture of intuition and systematic discipline needed for code breaking. After all, he had designed his mental Turing machine as a way to

Bletchley Park Today

After the war ended, most of the equipment at Bletchley Park was quickly dismantled and the thousands of workers resumed their civilian careers. The history of the facility and its achievements would remain secret until the 1970s. Meanwhile, the mansion and outbuildings were owned by a succession of firms including British Telecom and various government agencies. The facility was also used by the Government Communications Headquarters (GCHQ), for courses in cryptanalysis until 1987.

At the start of the 1990s, Bletchley Park was virtually deserted, the buildings badly in need of repair. The property was being considered for demolition and redevelopment. Fortunately, Bletchley Park was designated a protected site, and in 1992, the Bletchley Park Trust was formed to rehabilitate the site as a museum, which opened the following year.

In 2005, a donation by the American millionaire Sidney Frank enabled the construction of a new science center at Bletchley Park. The new center is dedicated to the memory of Alan Turing. Further expansion came in 2008, when the British National Museum of Computing was also established at Bletchley Park. Nevertheless, funding for expansion of the historic site has remained scarce.

Today, visitors can see a large-scale model of a German U-boat, a working replica of a Colossus code-breaking computer, as well as a replica of one of the earlier Bombe machines. Other attractions awaiting visitors to Bletchley Park include exhibits of Winston systematically transform one pattern of symbols into another. That was the essence of mathematical systems—and ciphers.

Turing could thus use his advanced mathematical knowledge to go beyond the rough and ready tricks of the traditional code breaker. From his earlier work on computable numbers (and perhaps Gödel's numbers representing mathematical statements), Turing developed a way to weight the probability that a given solution to the cipher was correct. Using Bayesian statistics (first developed by an 18th-century British mathematician), he could manipulate these probabilities and in effect sort them so the most probable patterns would be tested. This meant that ciphers could be solved far more

Bletchley Park today is a museum and science center where working replicas of World War II code-breaking machines can be seen. (Bletchley Park Trust)

Churchill memorabilia, vintage movie-making equipment, 1930s toy soldiers and model trains, and antique cars.

quickly than using the brute force of churning through tens of thousands of permutations.

Bletchley Park was starting to keep up with the Enigma transmissions, but they needed more clerks to process messages and operate the Bombes. Indeed, breaking the cipher, as difficult as that could be, was only the first step in obtaining useful intelligence. As F. H. Hinsley noted in the first volume in his monumental history of British intelligence in World War II:

Directing the Bombe

Position	1	2	3	4	5	6	7	8	9	10	11	12
Crib	A	T	T	A	C	K	A	T	D	A	W	N
Ciphertext	W	S	N	P	N	L	K	L	S	T	C	S

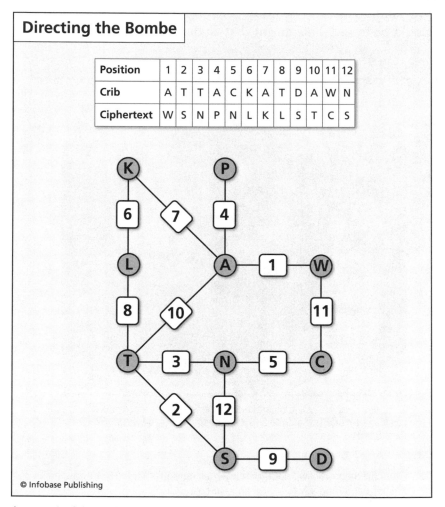

© Infobase Publishing

As a result of the statistical approach pioneered by Turing, a series or "menu" of possible settings could be derived and used to direct the operation of the Bombe, greatly speeding the decryption process.

*Apart from their sheer bulk, the texts teemed with obscuri-
ties—abbreviations for units and equipment, map and grid
references, geographical and personal code names, pro-formas,
Service jargon and other arcane references. One example is
furnished by the fact that the Germans made frequent use of
map references based on the CSGS 1:50,000 map of France.
This series had been withdrawn from use in the British Army.
Unable to obtain a copy of it, GC&CS was obliged to recon-
struct it from the German references to it.*

Hut 3 was where, in the language used in today's war on terrorism,
people "connected the dots," fitting the decrypted messages together
into a coherent mosaic of German capabilities and intentions.

Unfortunately, as valuable as "Ultra" (the code name for the
information obtained from Enigma messages) was, the actual use
of the information was far from efficient or consistent. Partly this
was due to secrecy: The users of the information could not be told
anything about how it was obtained. And at first, the information
was sometimes used too efficiently. After a series of German supply
ships were located from Enigma texts and sunk, it was belatedly realized that the Germans might conclude their code had been broken.
Fortunately, the paranoid Nazis drew a different conclusion—that
traitors among them must be passing information to the Allies.
Nevertheless, the British learned to use Ultra more judiciously.
Instead of attacking every submarine they found, they mainly used
their knowledge to avoid them. Or, if they did attack a submarine,
they first arranged to have a plane fly overhead and give the impression they had spotted it by chance.

Meanwhile, the workload at Bletchley Park was overwhelming.
At first, Turing and his colleagues made polite requests for more
workers, but skilled workers of all types were in demand by vital
industries such as aircraft production or radar development. Finally,
Turing decided to go right to the top, and wrote directly to Prime
Minister Winston Churchill:

Dear Prime Minister,

*Some weeks ago you paid us the honour of a visit, and
we believe you regard our work as important. You will have
seen that . . . we have been well supplied with the "Bombes"*

for the breaking of the German Enigma codes. We think, however, that you ought to know that this work is being held up, and in some cases is not being done at all, principally because we cannot get sufficient staff to deal with it. Our reason for writing to you direct is that for months we have done everything that we possibly can through the normal

A Desperate Plan

In the fall of 1940, Turing and the other British cryptanalysts were stymied by recent changes to the Enigma and had lost the ability to decipher the messages. One naval intelligence agent, Ian Fleming, proposed an audacious plan worthy of his later creation—James Bond. It read as follows:

I suggest we obtain the loot by the following means:

1. Obtain from Air Ministry an air-worthy German bomber.
2. Pick a tough crew of five, including a pilot, W/T operator and word-perfect German speaker. Dress them in German Air Force uniform, add blood and bandages to suit.
3. Crash plane in the Channel after making S.O.S. to rescue service in P/L.
4. Once aboard rescue boat, shoot German crew, dump overboard, bring rescue boat back to English port.

The Admiralty turned down Fleming's proposal. Frank Birch, head of the naval interpretation section at Bletchley Park, recalled that

Turing and Twinn came to me like undertakers cheated of a nice corpse two days ago, all in a stew about the cancellation of Operation Ruthless. The burden of their song was the importance of a pinch. Did the authorities realise that, since the Germans did the dirt on their machine on June 1st, there was very little hope, if any, of their deciphering current, or even approximately current, enigma for months and months and months—if ever?

Fortunately, several times during the war British forces were able to capture German Enigma material by more conventional means.

channels, and that we despair of any early improvement without your intervention.

Churchill immediately issued the following memo:

Action this Day
    Make sure they have all they want on extreme priority and report to me that this has been done.

Turing Goes Afield

Because of his role as leader of the attack on the German naval Enigma in what was known as Hut 8, many of the women volunteers also came under Turing's jurisdiction. Here he was, a 28-year-old man who had grown up and worked in an almost exclusively masculine environment. Accordingly, he kept his contact with the women employees infrequent and businesslike. Many of the women, though, admired the shy Turing and nicknamed him "the Prof."

There was one exception to Turing's minimal contact with women. Turing found it easy to talk with Joan Clarke—in part, perhaps, because she was a mathematician and thus a colleague, not just a clerk like most of the women at Bletchley. At any rate, they started going to the occasional movie together. Joan had developed an interest in chess, but she and Turing lacked a chess set. No problem—they obtained some clay and molded their own pieces, which Turing then fired at the coal fire in his room. The two also rode their bicycles around the countryside on days off.

In general, the workers at Bletchley Park worked very hard, and took what simple pleasures they could find. In his memoir *Chronicles of Wasted Time*, the writer and World War II British intelligence officer Malcolm Muggeridge (1903–1990) recalled:

Every day after luncheon when the weather was propitious the ciphers-crackers played rounders on the manor-house lawn, assuming the quasi-serious manner dons affect when engaged in activities likely to be regarded as frivolous or insignificant in comparison with their weightier studies. Thus they would dispute some point about the game with the same fervor as they might the question of free-will or determinism. . . . Shaking their heads ponderously, sucking air noisily into their noses between words—'I thought mine was the surer stroke,' or: 'I can assert without contradiction that my right foot was already . . .'

Turing's affection for Clarke grew, until he proposed marriage to her. She accepted, even though he had warned her that he had what he called homosexual tendencies. This was a far from uncommon experience for gay men of this era. Turing was still in the process of coming to terms with his homosexuality, and all the forces of his upbringing and the larger society pushed toward marriage as the expected outcome of a deep friendship between a man and a woman. However, the needs of the war would soon separate them.

After the Japanese bombed Pearl Harbor, and the United States entered the war against both Japan and Germany, the Americans found they were badly prepared for war. The United States had little experience with submarine warfare, and packs of U-boats began to gather off the American East Coast, tearing at largely defenseless cargo ships.

The Americans realized that they needed their own facility for decoding Enigma traffic to those submarines. The British agreed to send them their foremost expert—Alan Turing. In November 1942, Turing arrived safely in New York harbor. Having escaped the U-boats, however, he was nearly "torpedoed" by American bureaucracy—the British authorities had not procured the necessary entry papers.

After that little problem was dealt with, Turing immediately took a train to Washington, D.C., where he met with the assembled American code breakers and brought them up to date on codebreaking, machine style. The Americans, with their seemingly limitless industrial capacity, wasted no time. With the plans from Bletchley Park and Turing's personally delivered advice, a National Cash Register (NCR) factory in Ohio built more than a hundred large Bombes.

While Turing was impressed by American industry and by several of the researchers he met, in his report back to London about American naval cryptography, his opinion of his hosts was clearly less than flattering. After discovering that one cryptographer had been using statistical methods without understanding the principles of strength of evidence and probability, he wrote:

> *I am persuaded that one cannot very well trust these people where a matter of judgment in cryptography is concerned. I think we can make quite a lot of use of their machinery.*

In addition to advising the Americans on Enigma, Turing also found he could pursue a different kind of cryptography. Visiting Bell Labs, one of the nation's most innovative industrial laboratories, Turing conferred with engineers who were working on a method to encrypt speech. If successful, that meant that voice transmissions as well as Morse code could be used safely for military and diplomatic communications. Although the technical challenges for voice encryption were formidable, the techniques Turing picked up at Bell Labs would be put to good use later in Britain.

In March 1943, Turing returned to Britain by troop ship, no doubt hoping that his colleagues back at Hut 8 were keeping a sharp eye on the U-boats. (In fact, the Germans won their last major skirmish in the Battle of the Atlantic that month when several wolf packs converged on a convoy and sank 23 ships. The Germans had succeeded in some code breaking of their own—they had deciphered the instructions being sent to the convoys. The Allies found out when they decrypted the German Enigma messages describing that achievement and immediately revised their convoy cipher.)

After he returned, Turing could see Joan Clarke again, but time perhaps had let a realization sink in for both of them. Turing admitted that he could not be fully satisfied by any relationship with a woman, and she seemed to understand and accept this. The two would remain friends, though the closeness of their early days would not return.

Electronics Advances

By then, Hut 8 was running smoothly under its new head, chess master Hugh Alexander. Breaking the Enigma messages could still be challenging sometimes, but it had become increasingly routine. Turing was offered the opportunity to work on what one might think should have been a project right up his alley—the construction of a machine for breaking a different cipher, produced by the German Lorenz machine and called Fish by the British code breakers.

The first electronic machine had been called Heath Robinson (after a British cartoonist who drew elaborate but absurd contraptions—the American equivalent was Rube Goldberg). The machine used two punched paper tapes—one containing cipher characters from an intercepted message and the other containing possible wheel patterns from the Lorenz machine. The tapes traveled at 1,000 characters per second and often got out of sync or even broke. The optical tape reader was also unreliable, misreading certain patterns of holes. Thus, while the Heath Robinson was faster than the mechanical Bombe, its own mechanical problems limited its speed.

Max Newman (Turing's old math mentor) and the electronics engineer Tommy Flowers (1905–98) then came up with a new machine, called Colossus. Instead of checking a pattern tape against the message tape, it would generate the patterns completely electronically. This meant that only one message tape was needed. With no need for synchronization, the Colossus, which went into service in February 1944, could process 5,000 characters per second. (The faster and easier to use Mark 2 Colossus went online in June 1944, just in time for the Allied invasion of Europe.)

Although Turing did not work on the Colossus project, he was naturally aware of the details. Turing saw the big picture—Colossus was more than a triumph in code breaking, it was one of the first of a new breed of machines—if not the first—the electronic digital computer. As Hodges quotes from a technical paper:

> The analyst would sit at the typewriter output and call out instructions for [the operator] to make changes in the programs. Some of the other uses were eventually reduced to decision trees and were handed over to the machine operators.

The Song of Delilah

Turing, however, never liked being part of a team, and he gravitated toward a different project. In the fall of 1943, he moved to a facility at Hanslope Park, which was involved in communications research. Taking the ideas he had been working on in America, Turing began to design a voice encryption system called Delilah. Soon he was working with Robin Gandy (1919–95), a mathematician who had been a fellow student with Turing at King's College, and Donald Bayley, an engineer who also became a good friend, although Turing's revelation of his sexual preference would cause a temporary strain in their friendship.

The problem of voice encryption was fundamentally quite different from encrypting of Morse or Baudot (teletype) codes. The latter types of signals are discrete (easily separated) and digital. Voices, on the other hand, consist of an ever-changing mixture of sound waves. They are thus analog, not digital. A secure speech system had to digitize (that is, sample and measure) the waves to obtain enough information to be able to accurately reproduce the waves. The digital values could then be encrypted in such a way that they could be transmitted over a voice channel using a device called a vocoder, where they would sound like unintelligible static. The receiver, of course, would have to be able to reverse this process. Given the relatively primitive electronics of the time, this was a formidable challenge.

In March 1944, Turing and his team were able to encrypt a recording of a Churchill speech and successfully decrypt it. Delilah had appeared too late to be useful for the war. Nevertheless, the work broadened Turing's experience with electronics, which would be helpful for his later computer work.

As the year drew to a close, the end of the war was in sight. Germany was being pressed in by both the western Allies who had successfully landed in Normandy and a huge Soviet army coming from the east. Japan, too, had been largely swept from the seas, its navy virtually destroyed and its homeland coming under a rain of firebombing. (There, too, Bletchley Park and its American counterpart had played an important role, cracking the Japanese ciphers under a project with the code name Magic.)

In June 1945, a month after Germany's surrender, Turing was awarded the Order of the British Empire. Unlike other war heroes, however, he would not be allowed to say anything about the work that had earned the medal. In fact, though, Turing cared little for such recognition, and the medal went into a drawer.

Turing's mind was on other things. He had firmly grasped the possibility of the new electronic machines for making logical decisions and processing information. Code-breaking machines and voice ciphers had demonstrated a practical application for such technology. Now the imaginary universal Turing machine, with its ability to set up and solve any problem that could be solved, was about to become real.

The Birth of
the Computer

Like so many people whose careers had been diverted by the war, Turing had to decide whether to resume his previous course or strike out in a new direction. He thought about returning to King's College, where a reasonably secure life as an academic mathematician awaited. However, mathematicians traditionally used no tool more complicated than a blackboard. There would likely be little support at Cambridge or at most other universities for research on new tools and methods for computing.

While Turing pondered his future, he again took up his favorite sport, running. Turing was no sprinter, but he showed surprising power and endurance as a marathon runner. Indeed, he might well have qualified for the British 1948 Olympic team for track and field if he had not received a severe injury, serious enough to keep him

Turing boarding a bus with other members of the Walton Athletic Club in Hersham Road, Walton, Surrey in 1946 (King's College Archive Centre, Cambridge; the Papers of Alan Mathison Turing)

out of running competitively permanently. Even after his injury, though, he continued to run as a means of unwinding and collecting his thoughts.

In October 1945, Turing chose to go to the National Physical Laboratory (NPL) in London. This was a cutting-edge research institution, not an academic establishment. It was assembling some of the nation's best electronics engineers and was poised to pursue the new technologies that had emerged during the war, such as radar and computers. For the latter, it needed mathematicians expert in the theory and implementation of numeric computation. Turing was thus a prize catch for their new mathematical division—though he had to be hired only as a temporary senior scientific officer, at a raise of 25 percent more than his salary at Hanslope.

The official agenda for the mathematical division as established in 1944 included "Investigation of the possible adaptation of automatic telephone equipment to scientific computing" and "Development of electronic counting devices suitable for rapid computing."

Ironically, both these concepts were already out of date. While the British were building Colossus to break the German Lorenz cipher, another secret project had been under way in America. In early 1946, the Americans unveiled ENIAC, a huge electronic computer (with 17,468 vacuum tubes and 7,200 crystal diodes) that dwarfed the British Colossus, Unlike Colossus, which was specialized for code breaking, ENIAC was intended to address a variety of types of computation. It could spend a few weeks calculating artillery trajectories, then be programmed (by rewiring) to work on designs for a hydrogen bomb At the time, there was no other machine in the world like it.

Although it took them awhile to realize ENIAC's full significance, the leaders of the NPL saw that America threatened to open an insurmountable lead in the new field of digital computing. (In general, the British, whose economic position had been severely weakened by the war, were greatly concerned about their position in a postwar world dominated by the United States and its Soviet rival.)

Turing running in a race in December 1946 (King's College Archive Centre; Cambridge, the Papers of Alan Mathison Turing)

Colossus: a Forgotten Computer

In addition to the Enigma, the Germans used a variety of other cipher systems. One, the Lorenz machine, was used to encode teleprinter transmissions. Unlike the Enigma, where each message had to be completely encrypted and then printed or transcribed for sending, the Lorenz encrypted messages character by character by combining them with randomly generated characters using a Boolean XOR logical operation. The receiving machine could decrypt the message by generating the same sequence of characters and subtracting them from the cipher text.

Bletchley Park cryptographers caught a key break when a German Lorenz operator was told that his message was garbled. He retransmitted the message using the same key he had used before, but replaced some words with abbreviations. This allowed Bletchley code breakers to compare the two messages and figure out how the machine was manipulating the characters to encrypt the text. They now had a way to break the code, which they called Tunny. However, doing it by hand often took six weeks or more, by which time any intelligence gained would not be of much use.

A mathematician named Max Newman (who had taught Alan Turing at Cambridge) then arrived on the scene. Since breaking a Lorenz cipher involved comparing the wheel patterns they had deduced for the Lorenz machine with an encrypted message, Newman reasoned that a machine with logic circuits could read the pattern and the message from punched paper tapes and compare them far more quickly than a human could.

Their first machine, called Heath Robinson, read tapes at about 1,000 characters per second. It could not go faster without the tapes breaking. Newman then asked Tommy Flowers, an electronics engineer at the Post Office Research Station at Dollis Hill in London, whether he could do better. He could, and the result was the world's first programmable electronic digital computer.

Colossus had a key advantage over Heath Robinson in that it dispensed with the tape of Lorenz wheel patterns. Instead, it used logic circuits to simulate the Lorenz machine and generate the patterns electronically, which was much faster. (Tapes were still used for the encrypted messages being analyzed.) Instead of taking six weeks, a Lorenz message could now be decrypted in a few hours. (As with the contemporary American ENIAC machine, programs could not be stored in the computer. They had to be set up using switches and patch cables.)

Reporting for duty in February 1944, Colossus had arrived just in time. As the D-day invasion approached, it was used to read German

Built as a high-speed cipher-pattern scanner, Colossus was arguably the first electronic digital computer. (Bletchley Park Trust)

messages. There was good news: The Germans had been fooled by the Allies into preparing for an invasion of France near Calais. Thus, the real invasion in Normandy met with far less resistance.

By the end of the war, Bletchley Park had a battery of 10 Colossus computers, each filling a bay about the size of a room. The Mark 2 Colossus had 2,400 "valves" or vacuum tubes and could read messages at 5,000 characters a second.

After the war, the Colossus machines were dismantled, the plans destroyed, and their existence, like most of the work of Bletchley Park, was kept secret for decades. Fortunately in the 1980s, when restrictions had finally been lifted, Flowers and other Colossus engineers were free to talk about the machines. In the early 1990s, using their recollections and a painstaking analysis of the few remaining photos of the machines, a team led by Tony Sales of the Science Museum in London began the effort to construct a working replica of a Colossus. That machine was first demonstrated in 1996, and is still being improved.

Even today, most historians credit the American ENIAC (unveiled in 1946) with being the first general-purpose programmable electronic digital computer. Because of government secrecy, the British and their Colossus, although it had been built more than two years earlier than ENIAC, had lost its claim to fame.

The First Electronic Computers

ENIAC had shown the feasibility and usefulness of the electronic digital computer. However, ENIAC (at least in its early versions) was not easy to program. Turing had a number of ideas for a more advanced machine, and John R. Wormersley, head of the mathematical division at the NPL, gave him the opportunity to design a computer from scratch.

Turing's design (actually implemented by a team of engineers) would be called the Automatic Computing Engine (ACE). (The rather old-fashioned term *engine* evokes the Analytical Engine, designed, though never built, by Charles Babbage about a century earlier.) Turing presented an outline of the ACE design in a paper published in February 1946.

Turing's design for the ACE was ambitious. He was the first early computer designer to focus on making the machine as fast as possible. Turing identified memory as a key bottleneck limiting machine speed. In a 1947 talk to the London Mathematical Society he explained:

> *In my opinion this problem of making a large memory available at reasonably short notice is much more important than that of doing operations such as multiplication at high speed. Speed is necessary if the machine is to work fast enough for the machine to be commercially valuable, but a large storage is necessary if it is to be capable of anything more than trivial operations.*

Turing's proposed memory circuits, if they could have been built in their original form, would have operated about as fast as those of a Macintosh desktop computer four decades later. However, what was actually available for memory was something called a delay line. In the type used in many of the earliest computers, electronic data pulses were turned into mechanical pulses that traveled through a pipe containing liquid mercury. As the pulses reached the end of the line they were "refreshed" (shaped and amplified) and circulated back around. This meant that the data could be preserved indefinitely until needed. When a data item needed to be retrieved, the memory unit would wait until the right set of pulses came through the reader, which would convert them back to electronic form for transfer to the computers' working vacuum tube memory.

Despite Turing's insistence on the importance of having a large memory, the prototype ACE machine had only one delay line with 128 32-bit words of memory. Later, a magnetic drum memory with 4,096 words was added.

Turing had little to do with designing the memory. Instead, he focused on the design of the instruction set—the repertoire of basic operations, such as arithmetic and logical comparison. While the ENIAC "school" of computer design tended to opt for the ease of use of decimal number representation and favored building more elaborate hardware units for performing functions such as multiplication, Turing took the approach of simplification. He considered binary arithmetic to be perfectly natural for a machine that fundamentally is about "on" and "off" states (or 1 and 0). He felt that if decimal input or output is needed, programs could always be written to provide it.

In a 1946 memo now in the Turing Archive for the History of Computing, Turing commented on another proposed British computer, the EDSAC:

> *I have read . . . proposals for a pilot machine. . . . The "code" which he suggests is however very contrary to the line of development here [at the NPL], and much more in the American tradition of solving one's difficulties by means of much equipment rather than thought.*

Thus, instead of complex hardware, Turing favored a limited set of simple operations in hardware and then dependence on software routines to do whatever else is needed. In this, he anticipated the development of "microcode" for the microprocessors introduced in the 1970s as well as RISC or "reduced instruction set computing.")

Further, Turing designed the first complete "machine language"— a set of low-level instructions for arithmetic and logical operations, carefully tailored for efficient movement of data between the machine's processing units and the working memory.

Despite his explosion of creativity in ideas for computer design, Turing soon became dissatisfied with working at the NPL. He became

Who Was First—Turing or von Neumann?

The Hungarian-American mathematician John von Neumann (1903–57) was not only a mathematician but a "polymath"—someone who showed genius in a number of different fields, including mathematics (game theory and cellular automation), physical simulation, quantum mechanics, and nuclear physics.

Von Neumann was also an early pioneer in computer science. Although he did not create the ENIAC (credit for which goes to J. Presper Eckert (1919–95) and John William Mauchly (1907–80) at the University of Pennsylvania), he became involved in the design of its successor, the EDVAC. In his notes for the EDVAC, von Neumann described a key idea of the modern computer: the storing of programs as well as data in the machine's memory. This makes it far easier to create and modify programs, since no rewiring is required. However, Eckert and Mauchly had already written about this idea in an earlier EDVAC design paper, making it difficult to know how much credit really belongs to von Neumann.

Further, the idea of a "stored program" can actually be traced back to Turing's "Turing Machine" of the mid-1930s. Von Neumann was quite familiar with Turing's "Computable Numbers" paper, as quoted by Stan Frankel in Jack Copeland's *A Brief History of Computing: ENIAC and EDVAC*:

> I know that in or about 1943 or '44 von Neumann was well aware of the fundamental importance of Turing's paper of 1936. . . . Many people have acclaimed von Neumann as the "father of the computer" (in a modern sense of the term) but I am sure that he would never have made that mistake himself. He might well be called the midwife, perhaps, but he firmly emphasized to me, and to others I am sure, that the fundamental conception is owing to Turing—in so far as not anticipated by Babbage. . . . Both Turing and von Neumann, of course, also made substantial contributions to the "reduction to practice" of these concepts but I would not regard these as comparable in importance with the introduction and explication of the concept of a computer able to store in its memory its program of activities and of modifying that program in the course of these activities.

As quoted in his 1948 paper on "Intelligent Machinery," more than the other computer pioneers, Turing saw the true strength of the universal computer as being its flexibility:

> We do not need to have an infinity of different machines doing different jobs. A single one will suffice. The engineering

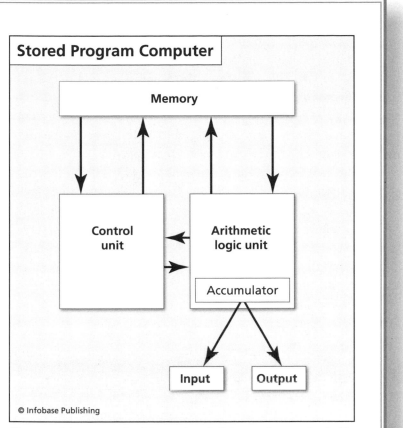

The essential components of the modern digital computer were implied in Turing's 1936 paper and further elaborated by Turing and von Neumann.

problem of producing various machines for various jobs is replaced by the office work of 'programming' the universal machine to do these jobs.

Not bad—Turing had foreseen the development of the software industry.

Although the popular mind firmly assigns a single inventor for devices such as the telegraph (Samuel F. B. Morse), the telephone (Alexander Graham Bell) and the radio (Guglielmo Marconi), all of those devices had forerunners and parallel inventors. The same is true of the computer. Perhaps the most judicious conclusion is that Turing was the first to describe the theory of stored program computing, but von Neumann expressed its engineering in a form that is still recognizable today.

discouraged and frustrated by having to be a manager instead of the "lone wolf" he always preferred to be. The ACE project constantly fought for adequate funding—Turing was used to Bletchley, where they had the backing of Winston Churchill to blast through any obstacles. At the NPL, Turing complained that about the time he had to devote to paperwork and attending meetings. Meanwhile, the administrators at the NPL seemed to have become equally frustrated with Turing, whom many considered to be temperamental and definitely, as would be said today, "not a team player."

When he was offered a sabbatical in 1947, Turing left the NPL and returned to King's College. This would effectively end his involvement with the development of the ACE, though he would remain publicly associated with the project and be interviewed by the media. (The NPL management began to view this with dismay, because Turing often used the interviews to talk about disconcerting things like artificial intelligence!)

Meanwhile, the NPL computer finally appeared in a reduced form as the "Pilot ACE" in 1950 and was marketed commercially as

Ace Pilot computer with three programmers. (National Physical Laboratory, Crown © 1950)

the DEUCE. (About 30 DEUCE computers were sold, despite that insistence by one of NPL's top advisers that three such machines would satisfy Britain's digital computing needs. A similar design would also be used for the Bendix G15 computer, of which 400 were sold worldwide, with some in use through the 1960s.)

A "Baby" Is Born

In May 1948, Turing accepted an invitation to join an innovative computing project at the University of Manchester. Their machine, officially called the Small Scale Experimental Machine (SSEM) but nicknamed "Baby," would incorporate significant advances in data storage and programming.

The SSEM used a new kind of memory device, During the war, the British engineer and inventor Frederic C. Williams (1911–77) developed a way to temporarily store radar images in a cathode ray tube (CRT)—the kind of tube used in most televisions until recently. To do this, he exploited the fact that each spot of light or pixel on the screen is accompanied by a tiny "well" of electric charge that could be obliterated by an appropriate signal. Williams's manipulation of the screen enabled the radar to cancel out images of static objects so the operator could focus on the moving objects that mattered, such as planes or ships. After the war, Williams had adapted what became known as the Williams tube so that it could store computer data rather than radar images.

The Williams tube memory used in the SSEM could store 2,048 bits (what would be called "2K" today) in a 64-by-32-bit array. (Since the SSEM used single memory units or "words" of 32 bits, this meant that it could store 64 data values.) While a glowing pixel in a TV tube fades after a moment, the data "pixels" in the Williams tube could be kept indefinitely by being "refreshed" with regular electronic pulses.

Following the Turing/von Neumann principles, the SSEM stored both data and instructions in memory. The instructions consisted of 13 bits representing the memory address containing the data to be used, followed by 3 bits giving the code for the type of operation to be performed (the other 16 bits of the 32-bit word were not used.)

With only three bits for instructions, the SSEM could have only eight different instructions:

Code	Instruction
000	Jump to the instruction at the specified address.
100	Jump to the instruction at the specified address *plus* the number in the accumulator.
010	Take the number at the specified address, negate it, then load it into the accumulator.
110	Store the number in the accumulator at the specified address.
101 (or 001)	Subtract the number at the specified address from the number in the accumulator and store the result in the accumulator.
011	Skip the next instruction if the accumulator contains a negative value.
111	Stop.

Looking at this table, one could see that the arithmetic that could be done by direct instruction was limited to negation and subtraction, though other mathematical functions such as addition and multiplication could be built up from combinations of these instructions. (For example, you could add a number by negating it and then subtracting it). The instructions that provide "jumps" from one instruction to another are particularly important, since they can allow for loops (repeated instruction sequences) and branches (different sequences depending on the value of a data item.)

A modern person watching someone program and run the SSEM would be quite puzzled about what was going on. Where we would use a keyboard to enter instructions and data, the SSEM had only banks of switches. And while our computer has a CRT or LCD screen with letters and numbers on it, the "display" on the SSEM consisted of the actual memory tubes with tiny patterns of dots representing the data being produced.

The pioneer British computer engineer Tom Kilburn (1921–2001) wrote the first program for the SSEM, which ran in June of 1948. Consisting of 17 instructions, the program was designed to find the

Christopher Strachey: Creative Computer Scientist

Born to a family of distinguished British academics, Christopher Strachey (1926–75) made pioneering contributions to computer science. Like Turing, Strachey had attended King's College in the mid-1930s, but the real friendship and collaboration of the two men began at Manchester with the work on the Baby and Mark 1.

Like Turing, Strachey had become interested in developing what at the time was called "machine intelligence." By 1952, Strachey had written a program that played a good game of draughts (checkers). One time, Turing played the machine. Because he understood its strategy, Turing beat the machine, which as programmed flashed "MACHINE LOSES." However, Turing was bemused when the machine then went on to insist "MACHINE WINS," thereby getting the last word.

Strachey and Turing also played around with a program that generated "love letters"—perhaps one of the first programs that processed text rather than doing math. Each time the program ran, it generated a new letter—for example:

DEAR SWEETHEART

MY WISTFUL ADORATION EAGERLY CARES FOR YOUR DE-SIRE. YOU ARE MY LOVABLE HEART: MY SWEET WISH. MY CRAVING DESIRE ANXIOUSLY THIRSTS FOR YOUR SYMPA-THY. YOU ARE MY CURIOUS DESIRE.

YOURS BURNINGLY
M. U. C.

Another of Strachey's innovations came about when he realized he could control the speed of execution of one particular instruction called hoot that was supposed to be used to sound a beep (such as for an error). Strachey used it to write a program that played "Baa, Baa, Black Sheep"—one of the earliest examples of computer music.

In his later career, Strachey focused on the design and analysis of computer languages, developing CPL (Combined Programming Language). Although the language was not widely adopted, its influence can be seen in successors such as BCPL and particularly the C language.

highest factor of 2^{18} (262,144) by trying every integer from 262,144 down to 1. (Divisions had to be performed by repeated subtraction.) To complete the program, the SSEM had to perform 3.5 million operations, which took the machine 52 minutes. (The answer, not surprisingly, was half of 262,144 or 131,072.)

In an article titled "Early Computers at Manchester University," Williams described this historic achievement:

> When first built, a program was laboriously inserted and the start switch pressed. Immediately the spots on the display tube started a mad dance.
>
> In early trials it was a dance of death leading to no useful result, and what was even worse, without yielding any clue to what was wrong. But one day it stopped and there, shining brightly in the expected place, was the expected answer.

Turing, who had arrived near the end of the project, could do little to shape what was after all Williams's computer design. Instead, he wrote programs both practical (such as a long division routine) and more esoteric (some of the first of what we would now call computer simulations, dealing with the biological patterns that were starting to interest him.)

"Building a Brain"

The successful creation of what many consider to be the first true stored-program computer was heralded in September 1948 by a letter to the prestigious science journal *Nature.* Meanwhile, the Manchester team had begun work on the Mark 1, a larger computer with features more practical for commercial use. One innovation of the Mark 1 was its use of index registers, special memory locations that could "point to" other locations, making it easier to store and retrieve data. The machine was marketed as the Ferranti Mark 1, starting in 1951. It and its American contemporary, the UNIVAC, showed that the computer was a practical way to organize and process large quantities of data for business, government, and science.

While his mathematical and logical ideas had been fundamental for the design and programming of the modern computer, by 1950

Turing had largely lost interest in the practical engineering of the machines.

Back in the Bletchley Park days, Turing spent some of his spare time speculating about the possible future uses of machines like Colossus. Later, in a letter in the Turing Archive, Turing explained that "in working on the ACE I am more interested in the possibility of producing models of the action of the brain than in the practical applications to computing."

Put more succinctly, Turing wanted to "build a brain" in order both to explore the ultimate capabilities of the machine and to better understand the essence of thinking and of intelligence. This topic, which would come to be known as artificial intelligence, would largely preoccupy Turing in the last years of his life.

Can Machines Think?

At least since the time Turing lost his childhood friend Christopher Morcom, he had been pondering the nature of the human mind and its relationship to the physical hardware—the brain. Was the brain, however biological its origins, essentially a machine? If so, then another machine—the "universal" machine Turing had first imagined in the 1930s, ought to be able to do anything the brain could do.

Of course the physical challenge of building a computer powerful enough to at least appear to think would be formidable. After all, around 1950 there were still only a handful of programmable digital computers in existence, and their combined power would be a tiny fraction of what can now be found in a "smart phone."

But creating a machine intelligence was not merely an engineering problem. It was also a question of terminology—what does one mean by intelligence, exactly? How could one tell whether a machine was responding intelligently to the problem given it? A logical first step was to find an activity that people would agree requires intelligence, yet that might be done by a machine.

From Turbochamp to Deep Blue

Along with a handful of other researchers, Turing hit on the game of chess as a way to build and test machine intelligence. Turing enjoyed chess all his life, though he was never a very good player. When most people think of chess, they consider it to be a pastime for people who are at least smarter than average. As for grandmasters such as the American former world champion Bobby Fischer (1943–2008), the popular image is of a super mind, although one often accompanied by an eccentric personality—not unlike the impression Alan Turing made on his colleagues.

As esoteric as it might seem, chess is quite simple in certain ways. The game creates a completely defined universe of 64 squares, over which only six types of pieces move in various ways. Although chess originated as a war game, there are no hidden snipers or ambushes. All the pieces and their capabilities are visible at all times. (Game theorists call such contests "games of perfect information.")

The core problem in tackling chess with a computer is that this little 64-square world explodes into a staggering number of possibilities after only a few moves. The player with the white pieces has about 20 first moves to choose from. In turn, the player with the black pieces has about 20 responses, the white player about 30 second moves, and so on. All in all, it has been estimated that the total number of possible chess positions is about 10^{50} (that is, 10 followed by 50 zeros).

Because of this more than astronomical number of positions, even today, a pure brute-force approach to computer chess is impossible. Turing knew this, of course, and the approach he developed was essentially the same as that used by every chess computer since, even the Deep Blue machine that defeated world chess champion Gary Kasparov in 1997.

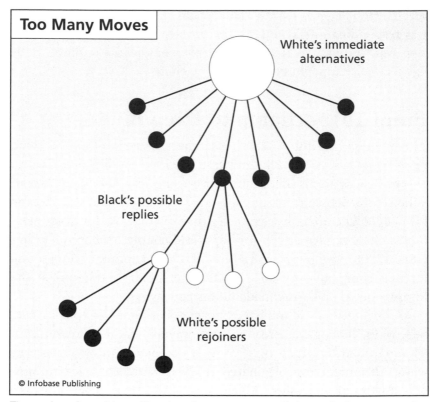

Too Many Moves

White's immediate alternatives

Black's possible replies

White's possible rejoiners

© Infobase Publishing

The number of possible positions in a chess game means that even the fastest computer cannot anticipate more than a few moves.

Two of the essential ingredients of a computer chess strategy are an evaluation function and a look-ahead mechanism. The evaluation function examines moves to see how much they improve the player's position. For example, a move might capture an opponent's piece or put one's own piece on a square from which it can control more of the board. Of course in chess it is also important to know what threats the opponent has—that is, what moves the opponent might use to improve his or her own position. By combining the evaluations of the computer's moves and the opponent's moves, Turing used a concept from game theory, called "minimax"—an idea pioneered by John von Neumann.

After evaluating all the possible moves and all the possible replies by the opponent, the program can generate the move that maximizes its advantage while minimizing the advantage for the opponent.

Do only this much, however, and one has a mediocre chess player at most. Good chess players can look several (sometimes many) moves ahead. (Masters may occasionally calculate a dozen moves or so.) To see why this is necessary, consider a sacrifice. This is a move where a player deliberately exchanges a valuable piece for a less valuable one. For example, the queen might take an opponent's pawn, even though another pawn can capture the queen in return. From the point of view of a very simplistic computer, this might seem like a very bad move, since it gives up the most powerful piece

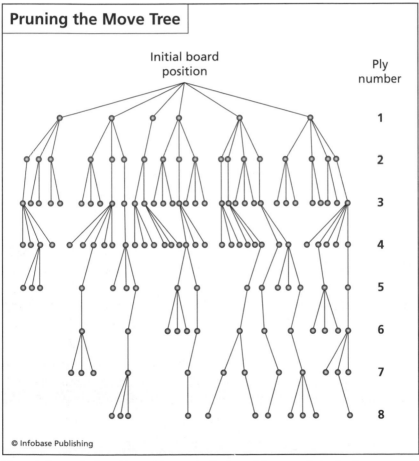

Pruning the Move Tree

Initial board position

Ply number

© Infobase Publishing

The solution to the "combinatorial explosion" of possible moves is to develop ways that promising sequences of moves can be identified early on, and unprofitable ones discarded.

in the chess army for a mere pawn. However, the player making the sacrifice sees that if the opponent's pawn takes the queen, it exposes the opponent's king to a devastating attack that will soon result in checkmate—and victory. To see this, though, one has to be able to look ahead two or more moves.

Early computers such as the kind Turing was working on had very limited memory and processing power, so they could not look ahead more than a few moves at most. In a paper published in 1950, the American computer scientist Claude Shannon described a third essential ingredient of a successful chess program—a way to prune or discard the many possible moves that were unlikely to be of any benefit. While this is something a human player does through ingrained knowledge and pattern recognition, a computer requires explicit instructions or algorithms to sift through the moves.

In 1950, Turing wrote detailed specifications for a chess program. They were so detailed, in fact, that even though there wasn't a computer powerful enough to run the program, Turing duplicated the program by hand, following its decision rules scrupulously and coming up with the resulting chess moves.

Two years later, Turing sat down with a friend, the computer scientist Alick Glennie (1905–2003). Turing played the part of the computer running his "Turbochamp" program against Glennie. In this first game ever between a "computer" and a human, Glennie emerged victorious.

Although computers played only beginner-level chess at first, by the mid-1950s enthusiastic advocates of AI predicted that computers would beat the best human chess players in only 10 years. In reality, it would take almost half a century, and the main reason why the computer would eventually prevail was not because it truly understood chess but because of the vast increases in computer speed, which has consistently doubled every year and a half or so. Combining a sophisticated evaluation function and reasonable pruning techniques with the ability to examine millions of possible positions per second, the computer eventually overwhelmed even the best human players.

But as impressive as today's chess computers are, AI researchers eventually realized that chess was not really a good test of machine intelligence after all. Chess programs got better mainly because

Turing, Robots, and Machines That Learn

Speaking about robots (an idea that at the time barely existed outside of science fiction), Turing told a Cambridge audience that:

a great positive reason for believing in the possibility of making thinking machinery is the fact that it is possible to make machinery to imitate any small part of a man. That the microphone does this for the ear, and the television camera for the eye are commonplaces. One can also produce remote-controlled robots whose limbs balance the body with the aid of servo-mechanisms. . . .

Turing suggested that such a robot, built using the technology of the time would

include television cameras, microphones, loudspeakers, wheels and "handling servomechanisms" as well as some sort of "electronic brain." . . . The object, if produced by present techniques, would be of immense size, even if the "brain" part were stationary and controlled the body from a distance.

In the coming decades, robots with considerable capability would be produced—and thanks to miniaturization, they could be human-sized or even smaller. But Turing's ultimate interest was in the hardest part to build—the brain.

In 1947, Turing wrote a groundbreaking paper titled "Intelligent Machinery" that would remain unpublished for more than 20 years. At a time when people were barely able to program computers to do useful things, Turing suggested that the way to get a truly intelligent machine would be to enable it to learn as a human infant learns. This idea was far ahead of its time—in the 1990s it would become the focus of a project at the Massachusetts Institute of Technology under the pioneer robot inventor Rodney Brooks. Today, a number of robots can learn by interacting with humans or other robots.

Most of today's robots, however, are restricted to particular domains, such as factories or hospitals. A robot, for example, might be able to pick up and deliver supplies anywhere in a large hospital, moving freely and safely among the human population. Such a robot, however, would not be able to play a game of chess or carry on an intelligent conversation about the latest three-dimensional movie.

they got faster, not because their "thinking" improved. They began to explore other tasks that required intelligence. As they did, they would find that Turing had already been there, outlining the key issues of AI in a series of remarkable papers.

The Turing Test

Turing notes in his 1950 paper on artificial intelligence that "if, during text-based conversation, a machine is indistinguishable from a

A person faces two unknown entities, one human and one computer: As they converse by teletype, the person tries to determine which is which.

human, then it could be said to be 'thinking' and, therefore, could be attributed with intelligence."

While working on the Manchester computers as director of programming, Turing devised an ingenious experiment to implement this idea—it would become known as the Turing test. The basic idea is to determine whether someone having a teletype conversation with an unknown entity can correctly identify the nature of that entity.

Interestingly, given Turing's own difficulties with gender roles, the original Turing test had the person try to guess whether the unknown conversation partner was a man or a woman. However, the most relevant version of the test for AI research had a person converse with two partners, one of which was a human and the other a computer program. The object, of course, was to determine which was which.

In his 1950 paper "Computing Machinery and Intelligence," Turing gives a sample series of questions from a human to an unknown partner:

> Q: Please write me a sonnet on the subject of the Forth bridge.
>
> A: Count me out on this one. I never could write poetry.
>
> Q: Add 34957 to 70764.
>
> A: (Pause about 30 seconds and then gives as answer) 105621.
>
> Q: Do you play chess?
>
> A: Yes.
>
> Q: I have K at my K1, and no other pieces. You have only K at K6 and R at R1. What do you play?
>
> A: (After a pause of 15 seconds) R-R8 Mate.

Each of these answers certainly looks like something a human might say. If, in reality, it is a computer that is answering, the program would have to be clever enough to (1) "deflect" the poetry question rather than attempt a rather difficult task that requires knowledge of poetic form, (2) give what is actually a not quite right answer to the math problem—a quick, correct answer might be a "give away" that a computer is involved; and (3) and (4) play chess successfully but not as a specialty—just one thing that an intelligent person might do!

In his 1950 paper, Turing suggested:

> *I believe that in about fifty years' time it will be possible to program computers so well that an average interrogator will have no more than 70 percent chance of making the right identification after five minutes of questioning. I [also] believe*

Passing the Turing Test

Back in the 1950s, few people had the opportunity to sit at a teletype terminal and go online with a computer. Today, however, much of the world's population seems to be spending many hours a day online, whether browsing the Web, reading e-mail, or sending text messages or "tweets." While most of the communications are between people who are simply using the computer as a medium, a surprising number of interactions are between people and computer programs.

Many of these conversations are with specialized programs that are designed to provide specific information or facilitate transactions such as planning a trip. However, there are also general-purpose programs that "hang out" on various chat systems and, at least at first, can sound quite humanlike. A "chatterbot" program might make polite inquiries as to one's health, discuss hobbies or other interests, even flirt or spread a bit of gossip.

Recently, some chatterbots with a more sinister agenda have appeared. They try to talk people into sharing private information or lure them to Web sites that promise prizes or peeks at pornographic pictures, but sneakily download "malware" (viruses and spy programs) to the victim's PC. Thus, it could be said that for some human computer users, failing a Turing test could be expensive!

Meanwhile, more formal Turing testing continues. A competition called the Loebner Prize (begun in 1991) annually pits programs against human testers and award prizes to the most convincing conversationalists. Although no program has yet won the top prize for sustained impersonation of a human, an annual prize is awarded to the program that shows the most progress toward that goal. In recent years, the most successful program has been the Artificial Linguistic Internet Computer Entity, or ALICE.

*that at the end of the [20th] century the use of words and
general educated opinion will have altered so much that one
will be able to speak of machines thinking without expecting
to be contradicted.*

Turing had also predicted the amount of processing power and
storage capacity that would be available in the computers of what was
then the distant future. In that respect today's computers greatly exceed
the wildest dreams of Turing and the other computing pioneers.

But AI requires at least as much development in software design
as in hardware specifications. And although some humans have
been fooled, at least momentarily, by some machines, the world
is still waiting for the machine that can meet or beat Turing's "70
percent" requirement.

Turing Begins the AI Debate

In his 1950 paper on "Computing Machinery and Intelligence," Turing
anticipated most of the questions and objections that still arise today
in conferences and public presentations about artificial intelligence.

The "theological objection" argues that intelligence requires a
nonmaterial component or soul that interacts with the body and
brain. Turing simply replies that if God can infuse a newly conceived
human being with a soul, He could equally provide a soul for a suit-
ably complex machine.

Another more scientific objection arises from the very same
mathematical problem that Turing had solved in the 1930s: that
of computability. Gödel had shown that any sufficiently complex
mathematical system contained assertions that could not be proven.
Would that not mean that any computer might be confronted with
questions that it could not answer using its logical programming?
Turing replied that even if humans (perhaps because of their more
flexible biological minds) were not subject to this limitation, the
mere fact that a computer might not be able to answer every possible question or give perfect answers does not mean it cannot think.
(After all, even the brightest humans get things wrong all the time)

A philosophical objection to AI argues that machines cannot
have an inner life with rich imagery and, particularly emotions. In his

1949 Lister oration, Geoffrey Jefferson(1886–1961), a distinguished British neurologist, argued that:

> *not until a machine can write a sonnet or compose a concerto because of thoughts and emotions felt, and not by the chance fall of symbols, could we agree that machine equals brain—*

Will Computers Ever Be Smarter than People?

Long a subject of curiosity for science fiction buffs, questions about the future of AI in our lives have already become an important research subject for think tanks. In September 2007, a conference convened in San Francisco to discuss what humans might expect 25 to 45 years from now as a result of advances in nanotechnology and the advent of smarter-than-human intelligences. The meeting was convened by the Singularity Institute for Artificial Intelligence and had about 600 "technosavants" attending, according to Ronald Bailey, science correspondent for the online version of *Reason Magazine*.

The idea of superhuman artificial intelligence is surprisingly old. The mathematician Stanislaw Ulam (1909–1984) recalled in 1958:

> *One conversation [with John von Neumann] centered on the ever accelerating progress of technology and changes in the mode of human life, which gives the appearance of approaching some essential singularity in the history of the race beyond which human affairs, as we know them, could not continue. . . .*

In 1993, the mathematician/science fiction writer Vernor Vinge (1944–) popularized this idea in "The Coming Technological Singularity." Vinge described the arguably inevitable time when the super-smart machine intelligence created by humans completely surpasses native human intelligence. This trend, it is argued, will be driven both by Moore's law (the doubling of computer power every two years or so) and by the fact that once intelligent machines reach a certain point they will be able to design improved successors without human assistance.

The Singularity Institute's concern, explains cofounder and AI researcher Eliezer Yudkowsky (1979–), revolves around ensur-

that is, not only write it but know that it had written it. No mechanism could feel (and not merely artificially signal, an easy contrivance) pleasure at its successes, grief when its valves fuse, be warmed by flattery, be made miserable by its mistakes, be charmed by sex, be angry or depressed when it cannot get what it wants.

ing that AI will be friendly to humans—a concept that the science fiction and science writer Isaac Asimov (1920–92) explored with his Three Laws of Robotics, which were designed to ensure that robots always place human safety and well-being ahead of any other goal.

Members of this institute generally belong to one of three schools: Event Horizon, Accelerationist, and Intelligence Explosion. Yudkowsky likens the Event Horizon idea to a black hole's event horizon, which blocks the view of everything behind it. Once the "Singularity occurs the future gets very, very weird," Bailey reports.

Accelerationist (and prolific inventor) Raymond Kurzweil (1948–   ) has described his view of the future in his book *The Singularity Is Near: When Humans Transcend Biology*, published in 2005. His vision assumes that humans will amplify themselves with the increased intelligence, so that super-smart artificial intelligence becomes part of the human condition and separate beings never get a toehold.

Again, according to Yudkowsky, the mathematician I. J. Good represents the current take on the third school—Intelligence Explosion. Because technology arises from the application of intelligence, a positive feedback loop creates a scenario in which self-improving intelligence bootstraps its way to superintelligence.

Of course the emergence of the technological singularity is far from certain. A collapse of human civilization from natural or human-made causes might derail it. Or perhaps one of the fundamental objections that Turing tried to answer might prevail.

The time line is also uncertain. Most singularity advocates predict that the singularity will emerge somewhere around the middle of the 21st century. But if the history of AI is any guide, predictions of true machine intelligence, including Turing's own, have often proven to be overoptimistic.

This objection says that computers cannot experience *qualia*—the term philosophers use for the subjective experience of, for example, the color red, as opposed to the mere reception of light waves with a certain length. Turing replied that no individual can actually prove that another person is having a subjective experience of emotion or of consciousness ("to know it had written"). If a machine can communicate what it says it is experiencing as effectively as a human, Turing argues that there is no reason to accept that the human has consciousness but the machine does not.

There are many other qualities or abilities that humans often seem to want to reserve to themselves as opposed to either animals or machines. Can a machine be truly creative? Can it be said to truly learn or come to understand something? Turing in essence turns the question back on the questioner. Who knows what machines of the future might be capable of?

Turing's Legacy in AI

Today, there is a flourishing field called cognitive science that draws upon many disciplines including neurology, psychology, and computer science. One thing that makes the field so exciting is the way people studying the human brain work with people who are trying to build artificial intelligences. On the one hand, brainlike structures such as artificial neural networks have been created in computers. Neural network programs, which have the ability to change their responses according to their success or failure (that is, to "learn") are surprisingly good at some tasks, such as recognizing faces of suspects in camera images. This, like the work with "learning robots" represents the bottom-up approach to AI.

A different approach is seen in projects such as Douglas Lenat's Cyc (short for "encyclopedia"), which depends on creating a huge database of facts about the world that a program can use to reason in a common-sense way. The creation of reasoning models represents the top-down approach

Perhaps closest to Turing's interests of the late 1940s and early 1950s would be the attempts to create machine models of the human thought and decision-making process. An example is MIT's Marvin

Minsky (1927–), whose career spans five decades and more, rang-ing from neural networks to his more recent models of human cog-nition and emotion based on what has been learned in working with computers and robots.

Thus, much of today's exciting research in many areas of com-puting can be traced back to ideas first discussed by Turing more than half a century ago. Unfortunately, tragedy and injustice would soon cut short the career of this remarkable scientist.

The Poisoned Apple

As the 1950s began, Turing's ever restless mind seemed to be moving in an entirely new direction—biology and, in particular, the study of the emergence of form as organisms grow.

As a child, one of Turing's favorite books was *Natural Wonders Every Child Should Know*. One passage in the book described growth like this:

> *So we are not built like a cement or a wooden house, but like a brick one. We are made of little living bricks. When we grow it is because of these little living bricks that divide into half bricks, and then grow into whole ones again. But how they find out when and where to grow fast, and when and where to grow slowly, and when and where not to grow at all, is precisely what nobody has yet made the smallest beginning at finding out.*

By the middle of the 20th century, however, at least a small beginning had been made in understanding the basis of inheritance and development. Indeed, in only a few years an American biologist, James Watson (1928–   ) and a British one, Francis Crick (1916–2004), would announce their discovery of the double helix structure of the DNA molecule, explaining how it could encode genetic instructions that specified the characteristics of the living "bricks" (or cells). By the end of the century, the molecular sequences that make up the complete human genome would be spelled out.

Patterns of Development

Despite this monumental achievement and the painstaking ongoing effort to link specific genes or gene complexes to traits and diseases, we are only beginning to unravel an equally deep mystery. While genes determine what protein molecules will be produced in creating a new organism, it is the complex three-dimensional folded shapes of these molecules that determine how they will actually function. These shapes are not encoded in the genes but arise from extremely complicated interactions between the molecules and their chemical environment.

Moving from the molecular to the cellular level, a variety of not yet understood signals come into play in embryology, or the study of development of organisms from conception to birth. As the organism develops, newly formed liver cells, for example, must go to the right place and attach themselves in the right way to form a liver. And most mysterious of all, the intricate migration and assembly of newly formed nerve cells (neurons) and supporting cells must create the structure of the brain.

In the 1950s, there was far less knowledge of genetics, molecular biology, and developmental processes than today. Turing, however, had been fascinated since childhood by the patterns that arise in the development of organisms.

Turing was particularly fascinated by the structure of flowers and other plants as he collected them from the countryside. One aspect that struck his mathematical mind was the way the arrangement of structures such as flower petals, branches, or the structure of certain fruits such as pineapples often matched numbers in what is known as the Fibonacci series (named for the medieval mathematician Leonardo Pisano, nicknamed Fibonacci, ca. 1170–ca. 1215, who first wrote about them). This series looks like this:

0, 1, 1, 2, 3, 5, 8, 13, 21, 34, 55, 89, 144 . . .

In this series, each number is equal to the sum of the two preceding numbers (1 + 1 = 2, 1 + 2 = 3, 2 + 3 = 5, 3 + 5 = 8, and so on). Although Turing had no background in biology beyond a school course or two, he was intrigued by patterns like this. In his 1952 paper "On the Chemical Basis of Morphogenesis," Turing concluded that there must be some regular series of chemical "waves" or patterns of reaction that resulted in the development of an organism's characteristic shape.

Turing especially focused on the diffusion, or slow spreading of chemicals. This would seem odd to many chemists, since diffusion in many cases leads to a uniform mixture and thus a loss of information that might be used to create patterns of structure. However, Turing showed that under the right conditions the diffusion of certain combinations of chemicals he called *morphogens* could lead to the emergence of complex patterns or structures. (This is rather like an example in physics—the diffused material after the big bang coalescing into whorls or streamers of gas that could eventually form stars and galaxies.) Turing wrote some computer programs to generate patterns that mimicked combinations found in nature, such as the dappled color "splotches" on cows. In doing so, Turing became one of the pioneers in using computer simulations to better understand natural processes.

Turing's growth model was one of the first examples of a "self-organizing system." Other examples can be found in mathematical structures called cellular automata, which had already been explored by the mathematicians Stanislas Ulam and John von Neumann. By the 1980s, researchers such as the prolific mathematician Stephen Wolfram (1959–   ) would be exploring in detail the connection between cellular automation (where each cell responds according to the configuration of its neighbors) and biological and other natural

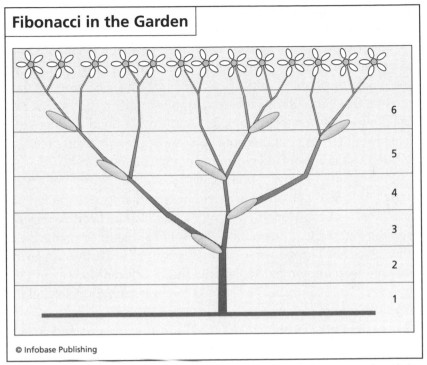

Fibonacci in the Garden

© Infobase Publishing

Turing was intrigued by the fact that many plants organize their branches and petals in accordance with the Fibonacci number sequence.

structures. (Had he lived, Turing would no doubt have been interested in these patterns as well.)

Turing's specific theory lacked sufficient detail to fully explain morphogenesis—which is not surprising given the quite limited knowledge of genetics and biochemistry in the early 1950s. Yet again, though, Turing had been not just years but decades ahead of his time.

The Code Breaker's Secret

As the 1950s began, Turing's personal life seemed to be settling down. After most of a lifetime of living in a room in a school, a hotel, or a boardinghouse, in the summer of 1950, Turing bought a small semidetached house near Manchester. Suddenly he had a considerable surplus of living space, as well as furniture, a garden—and neighbors. A couple, the Webbs, lived in the other half of the building. (Roy Webb, in fact, had been a fellow Sherborne student.)

The Webbs got along well with their bachelor neighbor, sharing gardening chores. Turing would sometimes be invited over for dinner, and he happily reciprocated by occasionally babysitting their son Rob. (He particularly enjoyed the opportunity to observe at first hand how a child's mind develops.) On the other hand, Turing's lifetime of indifferent housekeeping could not be easily overcome, and he had a woman shop and clean for him four days a week.

Possession of a private home gave Turing another sort of opportunity. As a gay person in a world where that sexual preference could not be acknowledged, Turing's social life had been necessarily sporadic and secret. For example, he would sometimes visit Paris or other places in Europe where attitudes toward sexuality in general and homosexuality in particular were more relaxed than in Britain. However, the relationships he found there were usually brief and not very satisfactory.

Late in 1951, Turing encountered a young man named Arnold Murray. Having grown up in the rough working-class neighborhoods of Manchester, Murray's background was very different from that of the educated, sheltered academic Turing.

Murray was down on his luck, unemployed, shabby, and malnourished. Turing was attracted to him and also wanted to help him. He bought the young man a meal in a nearby restaurant. After the first "date" they arranged fell through, Turing brought Murray home.

A Fateful Turn

At first, the two men seemed to get along well as they began a sexual relationship and seemed to enjoy spending time together. However, about a month later, in January 1952, Turing discovered that some money was missing from his wallet. Murray denied that he had taken the cash, and Turing believed him. He also began giving Murray small loans to help pay his expenses.

One night, Turing came home from a late session at the computer lab and discovered that his house had been broken into by burglars. Although little of value had been taken, the incident not surprisingly shocked Turing. Saddened and angered, Turing came to the conclusion that Murray must have had something to do with the break-in.

Murray denied this but suggested to Turing that because he had talked about Turing to some of his acquaintances in Manchester bars, some of them may have gotten the idea that valuables were to be had at the Turing residence. In particular, Murray said that one acquaintance known only as Harry had suggested that they break into Turing's house. Murray said he had turned Harry down, but now he suspected that Harry had gone ahead with the burglary.

Turing eventually made his peace with Murray but was still angry and frustrated. He wanted to tell the police about Harry, but they would ask him how he knew about him. This, in turn, would mean revealing his connection with Murray and quite possibly revealing their illicit relationship. Turing decided to concoct an alternative explanation that did not involve Murray. He went to the local police office.

But the police already knew about Harry, having found his fingerprints in Turing's house. When they questioned Harry, he confessed to the burglary but also told them about the relationship between Turing and Murray, perhaps hoping to strike a deal for a lesser sentence.

The police were not particularly eager to prosecute the respected mathematician for the crime of "gross indecency" (which included homosexual relationships). But when they started to question Turing and his story quickly unraveled, Turing decided that he was tired of hiding an essential part of his being. He admitted his relationship with Murray, including the details of their sexual acts. This left the police with little choice, and the charges were filed.

Verdict and Aftermath

At first, Turing wanted to fight the indecency charges, but his older brother, John, an attorney, talked him out of it. The evidence was overwhelming, after all, and corroborated by Turing's own defiant declaration to the police.

Instead, Turing's attorney, G. Lind-Smith, pleaded with the judge for leniency. As quoted by Hodges, he argued:

Homosexuality and the Law in Britain

The law against sodomy in England came down by formal decree from Henry VIII in 1533, making it a capital crime—that is, a civil offense punishable by death. That law, with its harsh penalty, remained on the books for centuries, with capital punishment enforced up to 1828, the only exception being a brief period in the 1500s.

During the 17th and part of the 18th centuries, however, public attitudes toward homosexuality were generally more tolerant. While sodomy had a wider meaning during this period—it was extended to include both same-sex and heterosexual sex acts not intended to be reproductive—offenders were less aggressively pursued, perhaps, than in other periods.

Not until 1828 was the act of sodomy downgraded to a felony punishable by imprisonment rather than death, and that lasted for the rest of the century. Meanwhile, with the support of the "social purity movement," an amendment was proposed to the law governing acts of "gross indecency" that would raise the age of consent for adolescent girls from 13 years to 16 years—thereby apparently intending to protect women in their early teens from sexual assaults at least until they were 16. The framers of the law did not target same-sex involvements at all, but enforcers later reinterpreted the vague wording "gross indecency" to include homosexual sex.

From the Victorian age of the late 19th century to the middle of the 20th century, homosexual relationships remained illegal. Such relationships were often accepted in certain literary and artistic circles, which also tolerated or even encouraged freewheeling heterosexual relationships such as "open marriages" with multiple partners.

In such circles, it was easy to believe that social standards had changed. Forgetting the strictures of the larger society could be disastrous, however. In the most famous British case, one which somewhat parallels Turing's, an unwise libel suit by the Irish writer Oscar Wilde (1854–1900) led to the exposure of his homosexual relationships, and eventually to his being sentenced in 1895 to two years' hard labor. (His health broken, he died in poverty in 1900, at the age of 46.)

By the mid-20th century, conflicting views about homosexuality were evident in both Britain and the United States. Most religious people and conservatives continued to support strict laws against what they considered to be a sinful way of life that threatened the family and social order. At the other extreme, a number of intellectuals of a strongly liberal persuasion not only tolerated homosexuals; they saw no reason why any form of sex between consenting adults should be any business of the state.

Oscar Wilde, about 1892—the travails of the 19th-century homosexual British author had similarities to Turing's own troubles half a century later. (Library of Congress)

Somewhere in between was the medical establishment, particularly psychiatry. Until the 1970s, the prevailing view there was that homosexuality was a mental illness for which treatment should be offered. However, no treatment, whether involving chemicals, electric shock, or psychoanalysis proved generally effective in changing sexual orientation.

Decriminalization of sodomy between same-sex consenting adults, as well as other consensual acts between adults, occurred in England in 1967.

[Turing] is entirely absorbed in his work and it would be a loss if a man of his ability—which is no ordinary ability— were not able to carry on with it. The public would lose the benefit of the research work he is doing. There is treatment which could be given him. I ask you to think that the public

Turing at age 39 (Time & Life Pictures/Getty Images)

interest would not be well served if this man is taken away from the important work he is doing.

The judge was not pleased by what he saw as Turing's lack of repentance. Nevertheless, he agreed that Turing would be given probation instead of prison time, provided he submitted to treatment. The treatment was based on the dubious idea that regular injections of estrogen (the female sex hormone) would shut down Turing's sex drive and make him lose interest in pursuing sex with men. Despite some unpleasant side effects such as breast enlargement, Turing seemed to take the treatment in stride. He continued his promising work on biological patterns. And since his travel was not restricted, he continued periodic trips to Europe, where discreet homosexual activity generally did not draw the attention of the authorities.

The computer side of Turing's work would be seriously affected by his conviction, however. Agencies that might have eagerly consulted him on cold war code-cracking problems were no longer interested. Turing's security clearance had been canceled, because of the belief that homosexuals were inevitably subject to blackmail by enemy agents. (The irony, of course, is that this was so only because of the harsh laws against such activity.)

Turing's Inner Journey

By then, however, Turing was much more interested in biology and patterns of development than he was in computer science as such. He also turned his curiosity to homosexuality itself. What made some people gay in a mostly straight world? To learn more, Turing went to a psychiatrist named Franz Greenbaum not because he thought he had any sort of mental illness, but because he thought that techniques such as dream interpretation might yield clues about what had shaped his own "morphogenesis."

The most popular psychological theory of the time, first introduced by Sigmund Freud (1856–1939), was that male homosexuality was caused by a boy having had an intense relationship with an overly dominant mother. While other schools of psychiatry had their own theories, most agreed to varying degrees that homosexuality was a form of deviant and pathological behavior.

That consensus began to break down in the 1950s for a number of reasons. Freud no longer had such a dominant position in psychiatry. Meanwhile, Alfred Kinsey (1894–1956), originally a zoologist, published his report *Sexual Behavior in the Human Male* in 1948. In his groundbreaking but controversial survey, Kinsey suggested that male sexuality was not a "binary" matter of straight or gay, but a continuum, and that a surprisingly large number of men had some form of homosexual experience at one time or another in their lives.

In 1973, the American Psychiatric Association removed homosexuality from its *Diagnostic and Statistical Manual (DSM)*, the official compendium of mental diseases. The APA's report stated that "homosexuality per se implies no impairment in judgment, stability, reliability, or general social or vocational capabilities." Two years later, the American Psychological Association urged that all mental health professionals "take the lead in removing the stigma of mental illness that has long been associated with homosexual orientations."

It is not surprising that Turing could not come up with a definitive scientific answer to the origin of homosexuality. Most researchers today can only suggest that homosexuality is likely to be a naturally occurring variation arising from some unknown combination of genes, hormonal balance, and environmental influence.

Turing's interest was personal as well as scientific, of course. Greenbaum, a Jungian analyst, did not share the Freudian view of homosexuality as a perversion. (The Swiss psychiatrist Carl Gustav Jung (1875–1961) emphasized wholeness and the integration of the personality as the goal of psychotherapy.) Greenbaum was sympathetic to Turing's desire to understand more about his personality. Later, the two went on from being doctor and patient to friends.

Ambiguous Death and Certain Tragedy

By most appearances, Turing had weathered the storm by the end of 1953. His probation and hormone treatments had ended. Manchester University had agreed to employ him for at least five more years. That summer, Turing enjoyed a trip to two of his favorite vacation spots—Paris and Greece.

Turing had also begun to widen his horizons as a writer. He wrote a story about the struggles of a homosexual man, echoing many of his own experiences. In some ways, he seemed poised to enter the wider world of intellectual discourse, a world in which scientists and people in the humanities often seemed to be talking past one another.

There would seem to be time for anything that Turing really wanted to pursue. After all, he was barely in his forties. While many mathematicians feel that it is unlikely for people to do great work in that field in middle age, there was the new field of computer science that Turing had practically invented. Beyond that there was artificial intelligence, filled with intriguing possibilities that Turing had already written about. There were also exciting discoveries on the frontiers of molecular biology, which was about to be revolutionized by the discovery of the role of DNA.

While traveling through Paris, Corfu, and Athens during the summer of 1953, Turing sent four postcards to his friend and colleague Robin Gandy. They included speculations and equations in quantum physics and an odd bit of poetry:

Hyperboloids of wondrous Light

Rolling for aye through Space and Time

Harbour there Waves which somehow Might

Play out God's holy pantomime.

And then, abruptly, there was silence. On the morning of June 8, 1954, Turing's housekeeper found his body in bed. On the nightstand was an apple with several bites out of it. The coroner ruled that Turing had committed suicide by cyanide poisoning.

Turing's friends later remembered that he had been fond of the Walt Disney version of *Snow White and the Seven Dwarfs*, which he had seen in 1937. Turing often quoted these lines from the animated film:

Dip the apple in the brew

Let the sleeping death seep through

Many of Turing's colleagues did not believe the suicide verdict. Turing seemed to have been in good spirits, talking about future projects and plans. No one could remember Turing speaking about the possibility of suicide, and he had left no note.

Turing's mother, Sara, had a different theory about her son's death. She believed it had been a tragic accident. She recalled how often he had engaged in messy chemical experiments, many involving cyanide. She also knew Turing liked to eat an apple before going to bed. Suppose he had gotten some cyanide on his hands, neglected to wash (not unusual), and ingested some cyanide while eating his apple?

Others did point to a few signs that Turing may have foreseen the end of his life. He had revised his will four months earlier. A few weeks earlier, he had visited a fortune-teller at a seaside resort. When he emerged, he seemed shaken and uncommunicative.

Further, proponents of the suicide theory suggest that Turing had deliberately staged his death in such a way that it could be interpreted as an accident. This would allow his mother to take some comfort.

A third theory related to Turing's wartime work, which was still classified top secret. After the war, it is possible that Turing had also engaged in code-breaking work related to the next great conflict, that between Britain, the United States, and their allies and the Soviet Union. (If so, however, no details have every been revealed.)

When Turing was revealed as a homosexual, the British security establishment broke off all connections with him. But quite possibly they worried that he might be blackmailed or enticed into revealing the secrets of code breaking and technology that had played such an important part only a decade earlier. These concerns were likely heightened only months before Turing's death, when a Soviet spy ring was uncovered at Cambridge. Two of its members, Guy Burgess (1911–63) and Donald Maclean (1913–83), had fled to the Soviet Union. Further, Burgess was a homosexual.

Today, more than 50 years later (and 20 years after the collapse of the Soviet Union), many secrets of the cold war have been revealed. However, if the shadowy world of spies and spymasters played a part in Turing's death, those secrets remain undiscovered.

There may be an indirect connection between cold war paranoia and Turing's death, however. During Turing's last few years, the anti-communist "witch hunts" spurred by the American senator Joseph McCarthy (1908–57) were in full swing. Besides suspected communists, homosexuals were a major target of this activity, to be rooted out and fired from any job deemed "sensitive." While Britain had nothing like the public uproar about the communist threat that had seized America, British intelligence officials were under intense pressure to accept security restrictions imposed by their American counterparts in exchange for access to nuclear secrets and other technology.

Thus, although there is no direct evidence, it is quite possible Turing's sense of isolation and depression may have been fed by the realization that he might soon be prevented from traveling abroad, including the European trips that enabled him to enjoy thriving gay communities. Naturally a travel ban would also have prevented him from attending scientific and computing conferences as well.

Conclusion:

Turing's Shrouded Legacy

Despite his profound and varied achievements, Turing's name would be little known to the general public until the 1970s. The breaking of the Enigma cipher and Turing's crucial role in that effort remained highly classified for almost three decades. As a result, histories of World War II largely neglected one of the most important factors in the Allied victory in both the Atlantic and the Pacific. Finally, however, the declassification of the Ultra and Magic code-breaking efforts led to a number of exciting accounts of the years at Bletchley Park.

Mathematics and Computing

Turing's great achievement in pure mathematics (shared with Alonzo Church and often called the Church-Turing hypothesis) was too esoteric for nonmathematicians to appreciate. The imaginary Turing machine used in that proof did not look like anything that would come to be known as a computer, though in fact it described the fundamental basis of all computing. The crucial concepts include a truly general-purpose machine, the storing of both data and instructions in memory, and the primacy of software over hardware.

Turing's role in the development of actual computers would also be obscured by events. His work at the NPL and at Manchester was overshadowed by the publicity given to John von Neumann's more or less equivalent ideas about stored programs, and the development of the ENIAC and its successors. Even the small British computer industry, built considerably upon the foundation of Turing's work, would soon be dwarfed by American companies, notably IBM.

Artificial Intelligence

In the artificial intelligence field, Turing's contributions were simply astonishing. He was the first to confront the question of how the computer could both challenge and help define the meaning of intelligence. He pointed out pathways to demonstrating AI (such as chess and text processing) and devised the Turing test, essentially a way to use human intelligence to test the quality of computer intelligence.

Turing's early and tragic death came just as the first significant AI programs were starting to be written. In 1955, Allen Newell (1927–92) designed a chess program that could learn from its mistakes (an idea that Turing had thought critical for the development of a truly intelligent machine.) In 1956, Newell and Herbert Simon (1916–2001) unveiled the first of a series of programs that could reason like mathematicians, creating surprising proofs for familiar theorems. That same year at a conference at Dartmouth University, the term *artificial intelligence* was coined, and Newell and Simon were joined by John McCarthy (1927–   ), inventor of the LISP programming language, and others who were working on AI projects.

What might Alan Turing have been able to offer to the burgeoning field of AI had he been alive in 1956? It is true that at the time of his death, Turing seemed to be focused more on his biological studies than on computing or AI. Further, as has been noted, it is quite likely Turing as a convicted homosexual might have been denied entry into the United States, or the British authorities might have even blocked his leaving the country. But if all those obstacles could have been swept away, Turing might still have had a great deal to offer in 1956.

While programming technique was advancing rapidly beyond anything Turing had experienced, Turing had something that few other early AI researchers could offer. He had a philosophical perspective that encompassed mathematics, engineering, and biology. He also saw the potential consequences of the development of intelligent machines and robots for society and the economy. (Norbert Wiener [1894–1964], father of cybernetics, could have been his partner in a wide-ranging dialogue on these topics.)

The Human Moment

To the very end, the life of Alan Turing is filled with irony. The greatest code breaker in history, whose efforts contributed so much to saving his country and Western civilization, would be rejected for breaking a rigid moral code. A visionary who saw technological possibilities decades ahead of time died just as he would have had the greatest opportunity to shape them.

The creator of the Turing test wanted a way to determine whether a computer might be able to pass as a human. But Turing was also his own "Turing test"—one that asked whether the humanity of someone who differed from the social norm could be accepted.

On September 10, 2009, more than half a century after Turing's death, the British prime minister Gordon Brown finally expressed an apology for the way Turing had been treated by the nation he had served so well:

> . . . It is no exaggeration to say that, without [Turing's] outstanding contribution, the history of World War Two could well have been very different. . . . The debt of gratitude he is owed makes it all the more horrifying, therefore, that he was treated so inhumanely. In 1952, he was convicted of "gross indecency"—in effect, tried for being gay. His sentence—and he was faced with the miserable choice of this or prison—was

chemical castration by a series of injections of female hormones. He took his own life just two years later.

Thousands of people have come together to demand justice for Alan Turing and recognition of the appalling way he was treated. While Turing was dealt with under the law of the time, and we can't put the clock back, his treatment was, of course, utterly unfair, and I am pleased to have the chance to say how deeply sorry I and we all are for what happened to him. Alan and the many thousands of other gay men who were convicted as he was convicted under homophobic laws were treated terribly. Over the years millions more lived in fear of conviction.

. . . It is thanks to men and women who were totally committed to fighting fascism, people like Alan Turing, that the horrors of the Holocaust and of total war are part of Europe's history and not Europe's present.

Statue of Turing at Alan Turing Memorial in Manchester (Aidan O'Rourke)

*So on behalf of the British government, and all those who
live freely thanks to Alan's work, I am very proud to say: we're
sorry, you deserved so much better.*

Turing Today

Today, fortunately, Turing's work has become known to the general
public as well as the scientific community. Andrew Hodges's popular
biography *Alan Turing: The Enigma* offers a lively, detailed account of
Turing's life and work. Documentaries such as the PBS Nova production "Decoding Nazi Secrets" explore Turing's wartime work. Even
plays have now been written about Turing's life. And, not surprisingly,
many homosexuals have embraced Turing as a heroic / tragic figure,
a man who struggled to assert his integrity in a hostile world even as
he looked toward a future in which "humanity" might encompass a far
wider range of experience, including even that of intelligent machines.

In 2002, a symposium called the Turing Day was held in Lausanne,
Switzerland. On what would have been Turing's 90th birthday, 250
participants ranging from scientists to a dentist who had become
intrigued by Turing's life, met to discuss the significance of that life
and work.

Today, we are all part of a universal "Turing machine" that even
Turing could not have imagined. The Internet seems to have infinite
possibilities, even if it often falls short in everyday use. Perhaps even as
this is being written, a human being in China is conversing with a program running on a server in Sweden. And perhaps in that exchange, a
Turing test is becoming a moment in which two kinds of intelligence
first recognize each other. If so, the possibility is in considerable part
the legacy of the unique human being that was Alan Turing.

CHRONOLOGY

June 23, 1912	Alan Turing is born in London, England.
1914	World War I begins.
1918	Turing is enrolled in St. Michael's day school.
1926	Turing enters Sherborne School.
1927	Turing makes friends with Christopher Morcom, who shares Turing's love of science.
1929	Morcom and Turing take exams for admission to Cambridge; Morcom passes with high marks, receives scholarship; Turing, a year younger, does not gain admission and must stay back.
February 13, 1930	Morcom dies unexpectedly of bovine tuberculosis.
1931	Turing enters King's College, Cambridge, on a scholarship.
1933	Adolph Hitler takes power in Germany in January.
1934	Turing receives his master's degree in mathematics from King's College.
1935	Turing, at 22, is elected a Fellow of King's College with the backing of John Maynard

Keynes, brilliant economist and member of the faculty.

1936

Turing's paper "On Computable Numbers" addresses Hilbert's Decision Problem, showing that it is not possible to determine whether certain mathematical assertions can be proven. Turing's paper also introduces an imaginary "universal" computer system that comes to be known as the "Turing machine."

1936–1938

Turing goes to the Institute for Advanced Study at Princeton University and works with logician Alonzo Church. Turing writes several important papers on mathematical logic. He also designs computer logic circuits and a prototype electric multiplier.

1938

Turing receives his Ph.D. in mathematics from Princeton University and returns to King's College. In the fall, he begins working part time for the Government Code and Cypher School (GC&CS).

September 1939

German invasion of Poland; Britain and France go to war against the Nazis. Turing reports to the GC&CS facility at Bletchley Park, where he works for most of the war. At Bletchley Park, Turing is effective in deciphering the Nazi Enigma code, an effort considered key in defeating Hitler's regime.

November 1942

Turing travels to the United States and works with U.S. Navy code breakers; he also helps Bell Labs build devices for encrypting speech.

Spring 1943

U-boats make their final major effort, but the Allies win the Battle of the Atlantic.

Fall 1943

Turing moves to Hanslope Park, where he helps design and construct a portable electronic speech encryption and communication device.

1945   Turing receives the Order of the British Empire (OBE) for his wartime work. Like the work itself, the award is kept secret for more than two decades.

May 8, 1945   Germany surrenders, and the war in Europe ends.

June 1945   Turing goes to the National Physical Laboratory, where he will spearhead the design of the Pilot Automatic Computing Engine (ACE)

1946–1948   Turing develops instruction sets, programming techniques, and routines for early computers.

1948   Frustrated by the slow progress of the ACE project, Turing goes to the University of Manchester, which was developing its own computer. He also begins to write a computer chess program.

1950   Turing's paper "Computing Machinery and Intelligence" establishes concepts and criteria for artificial intelligence still used today. The paper introduces the Turing test by which a person tries to decide whether the partner in a teletype conversation is a human or a computer.

1951   Turing is made a Fellow of the Royal Society, Britain's most prestigious scientific body.

1952   Turing's paper "The Chemical Basis for Morphogenesis" provides a mathematical explanation for the emergence of variation in the development of organisms.

Although no computer powerful enough to run it is available, Turing successfully demonstrates his chess program by carrying out its steps by hand.

Turing inadvertently reveals a homosexual affair to police and is arrested for "gross indecency." He is forced to undergo hormone "treatment" as an alternative to a prison sentence.

June 8, 1954   Alan Turing is found dead by his housekeeper; he is 41.

1956   A conference at Dartmouth University brings together AI researchers and in effect sets the agenda for the development of artificial intelligence. Turing no doubt would have been a key contributor to this effort.

1966   The Association for Computing Machinery (ACM) establishes the Turing Award in computer science, often considered the field's equivalent to the Nobel Prize.

1986   *Breaking the Code,* a play by Hugh Whitemore based on Turing's life, premieres in London.

1999   *Time* magazine names Turing one of its "100 Most Important People of the 20th Century."

2002   A BBC poll lists Turing as 21st on a list of the "100 Greatest Britons."

"Turing Day" symposium is held in Lausanne, Switzerland.

June 2007   A life-size statue of Turing is unveiled at the Bletchley Park historic site.

2009   Thousands of British people sign a peti-
                            tion calling upon the British government to
                            apologize for its treatment of Turing. The
                            British prime minister Gordon Brown issues
                            an apology in September.

2012   An "Alan Turing Year" will celebrate the
                            centenary of Turing's birth. Events will be
                            held in a number of places significant for
                            Turing's life and work, including Cambridge
                            University, the University of Manchester,
                            and Bletchley Park.

GLOSSARY

algorithm   a set of specified procedures for carrying out a task, such as a computation. A general purpose computer (Turing machine) can carry out any properly formulated algorithm.

analog computer   a machine that uses changes in physical quantities (such as electrical currents) to represent and manipulate data

artificial intelligence (AI)   the quest to create software or robotic systems that can recognize patterns, draw inferences, make decisions or plans, carry on conversations, or perform other activities thought to require intelligence and creativity.

binary number system   a number system that uses two as its base, rather than 10 as in the decimal system: for example, decimal 8 can be represented as binary 1000. In computers, the ones and zeros can be represented by the presence or absence of electrical signals, the alignment of magnetic fields, and so on.

Boolean logic   a system developed by the mathematician George Boole (1815–64) in which logical conditions such as OR, AND, and NOT can be manipulated algebraically. Early computer designers discovered that Boolean conditions were readily adaptable to binary (1 and 0) numbers and logic circuits.

bombe   an early machine for breaking Enigma ciphers. It mechanically stepped through a series of Enigma rotor settings, looking for ones that might yield a suspected plaintext from a cipher text.

chatterbot (or chatbot)   a program designed to carry on conversations with people over the Internet. They are often used to conduct impromptu Turing tests.

cipher   a system in which rules are applied to the letters in a message to transform them into a "scrambled" text. (This is different from a "code" where whole words or phrases are matched up with numbers or symbols.)

ciphertext   scrambled text that has been created by a cipher system

code although often used interchangeably with *cipher*, a code substitutes a number or text for a word or phrase in the plaintext, while a cipher substitutes letter for letter.

Colossus an electronic computer built to speed up the rate at which possible Enigma settings could be checked. Although not fully programmable, it was close kin to the modern computer.

crib a piece of ciphertext whose meaning is known or suspected, such as an introductory phrase

decimal the traditional numbering system, counting or placed in order by 10s; using a base 10 system

Decision Problem (German: Entscheidungsproblem) the problem posed by mathematician David Hilbert at a 1928 conference. It involves three questions: Is mathematics complete (accounts for all valid assertions); is mathematics consistent with itself, and is there, for every valid assertion, a method for determining whether it is true.

delay line memory a form of data storage in which data is stored in the form of acoustic or electromagnetic pulses that circulate through a medium such as mercury. The data can be refreshed so it is available indefinitely, but access is serial (sequential) rather than random (arbitrary).

Delilah code name for a speech encryption device invented by Alan Turing and a group of engineers at Hanslope Park

digital computer a machine that stores and manipulates data using exact numbers. Most modern computers are digital

electron a small, negatively charged atomic particle that orbits the nucleus of an atom and can be made to flow as an electrical current

Enigma An electromechanical cipher machine used by a number of countries, most notably Nazi Germany. The number of possible settings and the ways in which they could be scrambled made the resulting cipher hard to break.

ephemeris a table listing positions of the Sun, Moon, and planets over a given period of time in the future

Fibonacci numbers a series of numbers in which each number is equal to the sum of the previous two numbers. The series begins 0 1 1 2 3 5 8 13 . . .

finite state machine a machine that can have a limited number of specified states, each of which can be derived from a previous state, an input, and a rule. A Turing machine is an example of a finite state machine.

genetic code the information encoded in the structure of DNA that determines the creation of proteins in living cells and, broadly, the overall structure and capabilities of the organism

Halting Problem a version of the Decision Problem stated in terms of whether a computer program can determine whether a program will complete (halt) when given a particular input

instruction set the set of basic arithmetic, logical, and memory manipulation operations available in a given computer

integer any whole number, including positive, negative, and zero

Manchester "Baby" formally called the Small-Scale Experimental Machine; a small experimental computer built at the University of Manchester in the early 1950s. Its primary purpose was to prove the feasibility of using a Williams tube (CRT) as a main memory device.

memory the facility in a computer that allows for the storage and retrieval of data. There are many types of memory, some readily accessible and others large in capacity but slow in retrieval.

Moore's Law the observation by the technologist Gordon Moore that the number of transistor equivalents that can be placed in a computer chip roughly doubles every 18 months to two years. This has held true since the invention of electronic computing in the mid-1940s and is one of the reasons some futurists believe that machines will become more intelligent than humans around the middle of the 21st century.

morphogenesis biological process that results in an organism developing its characteristic shape or structure

neural network a computer structure that provides a simplified brainlike model in which connections are reinforced in response to the computer's success in solving a problem

Pilot ACE an experimental computer built at the British National Physical Laboratory in the late 1940s. Turing's involvement was mainly with programming and instruction design.

plaintext the original message prior to its being enciphered

plugboard (German: Stecker) a switchboardlike addition to the Enigma machine that allowed signals to be further scrambled, making them harder to decrypt

public school in England and Wales, an independent school that charges fees, usually offers a college-preparatory curriculum and, often, is structured as a boarding school serving only one sex; in the United States, a public school is a government-supported, free education provided for kindergarten through 12th grade.

program   a list of instructions for performing a task and written in a code readable by a computer

programmable   (of a machine) capable of being run by a program

Singularity   a time predicted by some futurists in which advances in AI, robotics, nanotechnology and other fields lead to the emergence of intelligences and capabilities that are beyond human comprehension

Strong AI   the belief that sufficiently powerful artificial intelligence can achieve humanlike mental states, including emotions and consciousness

Turing machine   a hypothetical machine, originally visualized by Turing to solve problems. It can use a set of simple rules and operations to perform complex calculations.

Turing test   a proposal by Turing that a human carry on a remote conversation with an unknown party that might be either another person or a computer. If the human cannot reliably tell whether the other party is a human or a computer, this can be taken as an indication of true artificial intelligence.

von Neumann architecture   the fundamental design of the modern digital computer, often attributed to John von Neumann but actually originating in Turing's 1936 paper "On Computable Numbers." The essential ideas are that the computer is universal, programmable, and able to store instructions in memory.

Weak AI   the belief that machines can be made to act as though they are intelligent, without making any claims about the machine's consciousness or inner state

Williams tube   a cathode ray tube (CRT) similar to that used in television, but in which the activated dots or pixels are used to store data. The result is a relatively fast random access memory that was used in some early computers.

FURTHER RESOURCES

Books

Bernstein, Jeremy. "A Portrait of Alan Turing," chapter 7. In *Cranks, Quarks, and the Cosmos.* New York: Basic Books, 1993.

> *A short, capably written biographical portrait of Turing, addressing, among other topics, Turing's homosexuality, a fact, combined with a stringent law still on the British books at the time, that filled his life with complications and tragedy.*

Copeland, B. Jack, ed. *Alan Turing's Automatic Computing Engine: The Master Codebreaker's Struggle to Build the Modern Computer.* New York: Oxford University Press, 2005.

> *A very detailed account of the work of Turing and his colleagues on the early British computer project that developed many ideas used in today's machines.*

———. *The Essential Turing: Seminal Writings in Computing, Logic, Philosophy, Artificial Intelligence and Artificial Life plus the Secrets of Enigma.* New York: Oxford University Press, 2004.

> *The editor's detailed and helpful introductions to each topic put Turing's papers in context, and bibliographies for each section point toward later work that developed from Turing's pioneering efforts in computing and AI.*

Crevier, Daniel. *AI: The Tumultuous History of the Search for Artificial Intelligence.* New York: Basic Books, 1993.

> *Describes the key pioneers and programs and their role in the development of AI from its formative years through the 1980s, with clear explanation of concepts.*

Garreau, Joel. *Radical Evolution: The Promise and Peril of Enhancing Our Minds, Our Bodies—and What It Means to Be Human.* New York: Doubleday, 2004.

In light of Alan Turing's deep interest in the human as machine and as "spirit," this book offers cutting-edge speculations on how technology such as AI, robotics, genetic engineering, and nanotechnology may transform human nature.

Henderson, Harry. *Artificial Intelligence: Mirrors for the Mind.* New York: Chelsea House, 2007.

Uses biographies of 10 key scientists to tell the story of the development of artificial intelligence from Turing's work in the 1940s and early 1950s to today's Internet "bot" programs and beyond.

Hinsley, F. H. *British Intelligence in the Second World War.* London: Stationery Office Books, 1996.

Abridged edition of a multivolume work that provides important background and perspective on the achievements of Bletchley Park.

Hinsley, F. H., and Alan Stripp, eds. *Codebreakers: The Inside Story of Bletchley Park.* New York: Oxford University Press, 2001.

Contains oral histories by 30 people who worked on the breaking of German ciphers during World War II. These interesting accounts became possible when secrecy restrictions were finally lifted in the 1970s.

Hodges, Andrew. *Alan Turing: The Enigma.* 2d American ed. Foreword by Douglas Hofstadter. New York: Walker & Company, 2000.

A revised and expanded American edition. Further amplified by an updated Web site maintained by Hodges. Available online: URL: www.turing.org.uk/book/update. Accessed September 19, 2007.

———. *Turing.* New York: Routledge, 1999.

Part of a series of short biographies of "great philosophers," this account provides a different perspective on how Turing's work relates to age-old philosophical questions such as the nature of mind and the limits of knowledge.

Kahn, David. *Seizing the Enigma: The Race to Break the German U-Boat Codes, 1939–1943.* New York: Basic Books, 2001.

Tells the gripping story of the race to break the German naval codes so British ships could avoid confrontation with German U-boats and successfully carry supplies to the island nation.

Leavitt, David. *The Man Who Knew Too Much: Alan Turing and the Invention of the Computer.* New York: W. W. Norton, 2006.

This shorter biography raises questions whether Turing committed suicide—or was it assassination? Unfortunately, the police closed the investigation quickly under the presumption of suicide. True, there was no suicide note, but there also was no evidence found (or looked for) that indicated otherwise.

Millican, Peter, and Andy Clark, eds. *Machines and Thought: The Legacy of Alan Turing.* Vol. 1. New York: Oxford University Press, 1996.

Essays by various contributors who continue Turing's exploration of the nature and limits of computation and intelligence.

Levy, Stephen. *Artificial Life: the Quest for a New Creation.* New York: Pantheon Books, 1992.

Describes how ideas about genetics, evolution, and ecology were combined with software to produce programs that could simulate the development of life forms, representing an interesting legacy of Turing's work on computational biology.

McCorduck, Pamela. *Machines Who Think: A Personal Inquiry into the History and Prospects of Artificial Intelligence.* 2d ed. Natick, Mass.: A. K. Peters, 2004.

Revised edition of a classic, engaging account of the people and achievements that have shaped artificial intelligence. Includes interviews with many of the field's pioneers.

Petzold, Charles. *The Annotated Turing: A Guided Tour through Alan Turing's Historic Paper on Computability and the Turing Machine.* Indianapolis, Ind.: Wiley, 2008.

Presents Turing's seminal paper with background and step-by-step explanations; accessible to readers with some basic background in mathematical logic and a willingness to follow the intricate steps by which the Turing machine reaches its conclusions.

Smith, Michael. *Station X: Decoding Nazi Secrets.* New York: TV Books, 1999.

Smith, a former member of the Intelligence Corps in England, writes authoritatively about the team effort required for breaking the German codes.

Strathern, Paul. "Turing and the Computer." In *The Big Idea.* New York: Quality Paperback Book Club, 1999.

A breezy account of Turing's life and key contributions to the concepts that together enabled digital computing. Includes an account of the history and chronology of calculating and computing machines.

Teuscher, Christof, ed. *Alan Turing: Life and Legacy of a Great Thinker.* New York: Springer, 2003.

A collection of articles by computer scientists and others reflecting on the significance of Turing's work as well as papers presenting new developments such as ways to pass the Turing test and the building of quantum computers. Some writers speculate on how Turing's career might have progressed and contributed to the development of artificial intelligence in the 1950s and beyond.

Whitemore, Hugh. *Breaking the Code: A Play.* Garden City, N.Y.: Fireside Theatre, 1987.

The story of Alan Turing—from his wartime successes as a code breaker to his tragic death—written for the theater.

Internet Resources

Bailey, Ronald. "Will Super Smart Artificial Intelligences Keep Humans Around as Pets? September 11, 2007. Available online. URL: http://reason.com/archives/2007/09/11/will-super-smart-artificial-in. Accessed April 2, 2010.

Report on the "Singularity Summit," where researchers and futurists debate the possibility that artificial intelligences will surpass human cognition while human brains are also enhanced.

Bletchley Park, National Codes Centre. Available online. URL: http://www.bletchleypark.org.uk/ Accessed March 1, 2010.

Provides a variety of background information about the historic site where Turing and other code breakers won their secret war against Germany. Visitors can see a working "Bombe" and a replica of the more advanced Colossus electronic codebreaking computer.

Buckland, Richard. The Amazing Alan Turing. Available online. URL: http://www.youtube.com/watch?v=2bLCjMA0YlE. Accessed March 28, 2010.

A professor at the University of New South Wales (Australia) gives a lively lecture about the three key contributions of Alan Turing to computer science. (Some of the factual details of Turing's life are inaccurate, though.)

Chess game, Alan Turing vs. Alick Glennie. Available online. URL: http://www.chessgames.com/perl/chessgame?gid=1356927 Accessed March 3, 2010.

Presents the first game between human and "computer," where Turing stepped through his chess algorithm, playing the role of the computer, since a suitable machine did not yet exist. The "computer" loses.

Copeland, Jack. A Brief History of Computing. Available online. URL: http://www.alanturing.net/turing_archive/pages/Reference%20 Articles/BriefHistofComp.html# ACE Accessed January 10, 2010.

Describes the development of key design concepts of the modern computer, with discussion of machines including Colossus, Turing's ACE and the American ENIAC and EDVAC.

Decoding Nazi Secrets. Available online. URL: http://www.pbs.org/ wgbh/nova/decoding/index.html. Accessed April 2, 2010.

Companion Web site to the two-hour NOVA television special that chronicles the struggle to break the Enigma cipher. (The program was first broadcast November 9, 1999.)

Hodges, Andrew. Alan Turing Home Page. Available online. URL: www. turing.org.uk/turing/index.html. Accessed September 19, 2007.

Hodges maintains this vast Web site, including: a short online biography, Alan Turing Internet Scrapbook, thoughts about philosophy, Turing Sources (archives and photographs, complete bibliography, original documents), and recent papers and articles by Andrew Hodges.

Loebner Prize Home Page. Available online. URL: http://www.loebner. net/Prizef/loebner-prize.html. Accessed March 10, 2010.

Provides information about the annual contest in which a $2,000 prize is given to the most humanlike computer program, including transcripts of conversations with the leading "chatbots."

Manchester Mark 1 Emulator. Available online. URL: http://alpha60. de/research/muc/ Accessed March 27, 2010.

Demonstrates the operation of the Mark 1 with a Java plugin. The example program is Christopher Strachey's Love Letter generator (1952).

Three Rotor Enigma Simulation. Available online. URL: http://enig-maco.de/_fs/index-enigma.html Accessed March 1, 2010.

Simulates the operation of an Enigma machine

Turing, Alan. "Computing Machinery and Intelligence." (From *Mind* 59, 433–460 (1950). Available online. URL: http://www.loebner.net/ Prizef/TuringArticle.html. Accessed March 27, 2010.

Turing's paper describing the original form of the Turing test and giving background and research strategies for machine intelligence.

Turing Digital Archive, The. Available online. URL: http://www.tur-ingarchive.org/ Accessed January 15, 2010.

Contains unpublished writings of Alan Turing, including letters and other personal papers, photographs, and obituaries written by colleagues. (The originals are in the Turing Archive in King's College, Cambridge.)

Turing Hub, The. Available online. URL: http://www.turinghub.com/ Accessed February 12, 2010.

Allows visitors to conduct their own Turing test by being connected to "someone" who may be either a human being or a "chatterbot" program.

INDEX